T0318327

'If you are looking for rigorous, accessible and bracingly contemporary answers to the "what", "how" and "why" of performance studies, you will find them in *Performance Studies: The Basics*. This meticulous introduction outlines the field's complex and contested genealogies, its theoretical infrastructures and its methodological possibilities. It efficiently and evocatively captures performance studies' scope, models its ethical commitments, and details its diversity: a "must-read" for students and faculty from high school to grad school.'
— *Judith Hamera, Princeton University*

PERFORMANCE STUDIES
THE BASICS

Performance Studies: The Basics offers an overview of the multiple, often overlapping definitions of performance, from performance art, performance as everyday life, and rituals, to the performative dimensions of identity, such as gender, race and sexuality.

This book defines the interdisciplinary field of performance studies as it has evolved over the past four decades at the intersection of academic scholarship and artistic and activist practices. It discusses performance as an important means of communicating and of understanding the world, highlighting its intersections with critical theory and arguing for the importance of performance in the study of human behaviour and social practices.

Complete with a helpful glossary and bibliography, as well as suggestions for further reading, this book is an ideal starting point for those studying performance studies as well as for general readers with an interest in the subject.

Andreea S. Micu is an Associate Researcher at the Mahindra Humanities Center, Harvard University. She has taught classes in performance, culture and communication at Northwestern University, where she also obtained her doctoral degree in Performance Studies. Her writing about performance has appeared in both scholarly and general publications such as *pARTicipatory urbanisms*, *Performance Philosophy* and *The New Alphabet School*.

THE BASICS

The Basics is a highly successful series of accessible guidebooks which provide an overview of the fundamental principles of a subject area in a jargon-free and undaunting format.

Intended for students approaching a subject for the first time, the books both introduce the essentials of a subject and provide an ideal springboard for further study. With over fifty titles spanning subjects from artificial intelligence (AI) to women's studies, *The Basics* are an ideal starting point for students seeking to understand a subject area.

Each text comes with recommendations for further study and gradually introduces the complexities and nuances within a subject.

NARRATIVE
BRONWEN THOMAS

PANDEMICS
ELISA PIERI

POETRY (THIRD EDITION)
JEFFREY WAINWRIGHT

POVERTY
BENT GREVE

THE QUR'AN (SECOND EDITION)
MASSIMO CAMPANINI

RESEARCH METHODS (SECOND EDITION)
NICHOLAS WALLIMAN

SEMIOTICS
DANIEL CHANDLER

SUSTAINABILITY (SECOND EDITION)
PETER JACQUES

TRANSLATION
JULIANE HOUSE

TOWN PLANNING
TONY HALL

WOMEN'S STUDIES (SECOND EDITION)
BONNIE G. SMITH

ENGLISH GRAMMAR
MICHAEL MCCARTHY

PERFORMANCE STUDIES
ANDREEA S. MICU

For a full list of titles in this series, please visit www.routledge.com/The-Basics/book-series/B

PERFORMANCE STUDIES

THE BASICS

Andreea S. Micu

Routledge
Taylor & Francis Group

LONDON AND NEW YORK

First published 2022
by Routledge
2 Park Square, Milton Park, Abingdon, Oxon OX14 4RN

and by Routledge
605 Third Avenue, New York, NY 10158

Routledge is an imprint of the Taylor & Francis Group, an informa business

British Library Cataloguing-in-Publication Data
A catalogue record for this book is available from the British Library

Library of Congress Cataloging-in-Publication Data
Names: Micu, Andreea S., author.
Title: Performance studies : the basics / Andreea S. Micu.
Description: Abingdon, Oxon ; New York, NY : Routledge, 2022. |
Series: The basics | Includes bibliographical references and index.
Identifiers: LCCN 2021017559 (print) | LCCN 2021017560 (ebook) |
ISBN 9780367232979 (hardback) | ISBN 9780367251758 (paperback) |
ISBN 9780429286377 (ebook)
Subjects: LCSH: Performing arts. | Performance art.
Classification: LCC PN1584 .M44 2022 (print) |
LCC PN1584 (ebook) | DDC 790.2–dc23
LC record available at https://lccn.loc.gov/2021017559
LC ebook record available at https://lccn.loc.gov/2021017560

ISBN: 978-0-367-23297-9 (hbk)
ISBN: 978-0-367-25175-8 (pbk)
ISBN: 978-0-429-28637-7 (ebk)

DOI: 10.4324/9780429286377

Typeset in Bembo
by Newgen Publishing UK

CONTENTS

ACKNOWLEDGEMENTS

This book would not exist without the help of Kelly Chung, the support of Elliot Heilman, the guidance of D. Soyini Madison and the students in my performance classes at Northwestern University, who taught me how to speak of performance in lay terms without sacrificing complexity or precision. To all of them, thank you!

INTRODUCTION

When we hear the word *performance*, we tend to think about staged or artistic practices, but performance more broadly constitutes an essential part of human behaviour and social dynamics, reaching well beyond the carefully curated events we might see in a theatre or art gallery. A sports game, a fashion show, a political protest, a religious ceremony, a shared meal and a military parade might at first sight strike us as very different events from a theatre play or a performance piece happening in an art gallery, yet all of these examples are physical actions in which particular aesthetic choices are deployed, social values are foregrounded and imaginations are forged. As humans, we *perform* constantly, and as we will see in the next few chapters, our performances shape our identities, our positions within social arrangements and hierarchies and our culturally shared values and worldviews. Human beings perform for a range of reasons, such as to communicate, entertain, reaffirm a sense of belonging, negotiate identity, transform conflict, make sense of history and imagine the future. Because performance lies at the very core of who we are as a species, some social scientists have argued that *homo sapiens* is, in fact, *homo performans*.

As an initial definition – one that we will probe and expand on in the chapters to come – a performance is a particular behaviour with a communicative purpose and an explicit or implied audience. Given that humans are social animals, our actions and behaviours are rarely only individual matters. We learn to perform from witnessing others' performances and repeating them. As we do so, we not only

DOI: 10.4324/9780429286377-1

imitate behaviours, but also transform them. This is, for example, how we learn to speak, play sports, or dance. We repeat and we create, and others learn to perform from us. This essential mechanism is hardwired in our brains and bodies to the extent that a great part of our performance is involuntary, such as when we repeat the gestures, mannerisms, or speech patterns that we pick from the people with whom we spend a lot of time. Oftentimes, however, we perform with a deliberate purpose: dressing up for a professional meeting, trying to look engaged while sitting through a boring class, or telling a compelling story to our friends. Whether we are aware that we perform or not, performance is the social transmission of information and knowledge using the body as a medium.

Many traditions, collective memories and histories are transmitted body to body through performance, even though official historical records have tended to erase these forms of knowledge transmission as backwards and primitive. Oral traditions and storytelling in non-Western societies have transmitted people's local histories for centuries. Even without written records, storytelling was the medium through which knowledge passed from one generation to the next. Starting in the fifteenth and sixteenth centuries, European colonialism helped expand the notion that only knowledge transmitted through written text was important – at the expense of these other forms of knowledge that were not written but were important amongst colonized people. In the centuries that followed, many forms of struggle against abusive power have used performance to transmit the histories of the oppressed alongside hope for future possibilities of freedom. During slavery, the American black spiritual 'Go Down Moses' used the Biblical story of the exodus of Jewish slaves from Egypt to talk about desires for liberation in ways that could slide under the radar of the white slave-owning class. The martial arts practice that we know today as Capoeira originated amongst Afro-Brazilian slaves adapting African forms of ritual warfare dance that allowed fugitive slaves to not only rehearse fighting techniques but also build a spiritual connection with ancestors from which they could derive a sense of pride and courage. Such forms of performance were in part successful in building resistance precisely because the culture of the European colonizers dismissed the capacity of the body to transmit knowledge. Because of its attention to the capacities of the body to build and share cultural meanings beyond written texts, the field of performance studies incorporates the voices and experiences of social groups that have been traditionally deemed 'primitive' or 'irrelevant' in Western culture and historical records. In doing so, performance studies shows us that our view of what it means to be human is limited when we look at history only from the perspective of the Western world.

By and large, the mistrust of the body as an essential instrument of knowledge still dominates our contemporary global culture, even though capitalism constantly needs forms of performance that it can commodify and sell. This process of commodification happens, for example, when companies recycle performances that are perceived as 'edgy' or 'radical' in political life and popular culture in order to sell products. The recent controversy over a Pepsi commercial campaign inspired by Black Lives Matter protests that featured model Kendall Jenner handing a can of the soft drink to a police officer illustrates this tendency. The ad made reference to Black Lives Matter but completely altered the fact that one of these protest performances' main goals is to call attention to the violence police use against black people. Performances can travel through multiple media channels, and in the process can transform into something very different from their original intent.

This book examines performance in its multiple yet overlapping senses. From the performing arts to social and religious rituals, historical re-enactments, everyday actions and performances of gender, sexuality and race, performance cuts across a broad range of human behaviour. The limits of what counts as performance are not fixed, and multiple phenomena have been defined and studied as such in the past five decades from the perspective of performance studies. Because performance comprises a wide range of phenomena, the field of performance studies both shares research interests with and diverges from other fields of knowledge such as theatre studies, cultural studies, dance studies, critical race and ethnic studies, gender and queer studies, media studies, cultural anthropology and art history, among others. This book introduces the reader to some of the phenomena that we call performance and provides an overview of the interdisciplinary field of research that is performance studies.

1

WHAT IS PERFORMANCE?

FRAMING PERFORMANCE

Although we commonly understand theatre and performance art to be quite different from self-presentational behaviour or ritual, and that both of those categories are very different from performances of, for example, gender, one of the goals of this book is to explore the porous boundaries between all those different phenomena we call performance.

In the art world, performance took special relevance in the 1960s and 1970s. *Performance art*, also referred to as *live art* or *body art* emerged at the same time as many artists were pushing the boundaries of the art world, which they considered to be trite, conservative and unable to respond to contemporary historical challenges. Even as they were mixing genres by combining visual art, painting, sculpture or dance, these artists were claiming the body as the essential instrument of art making. Pioneer feminist performers such as Rachel Rosenthal (1926–2015) or Carolee Schneemann (1939–2019) also called out the misogynistic culture of the art world and the secondary place it gave to women artists. Many performance artists of the time also advocated for taking performance art out of the traditional art and theatrical spaces in order to find broader audiences. These concerns with the body and the space of the performance have been characteristic of performance art ever since.

But performance art's tendency to constantly push the boundaries of what the appropriate places for performance are and who could be considered a performer have also made it more complicated to define performance in general. When performance art leaves the

DOI: 10.4324/9780429286377-2

space of the museum, the theatre, or the art gallery and enters other public spaces, expectations about how bodies should behave in these spaces are disrupted and the limits between make-believe and the everyday become blurry. However, precisely because of this ability to cross boundaries, performance has become deeply intertwined with various forms of political protest and activism over the past few decades. The relationship between performance and political protest has a long and rich history. In 1967, amidst widespread sentiment against the Vietnam War, a group of several hundred political activists led by Abbie Hoffman (1936–89) marched towards the Pentagon with the intention of staging an exorcism. Holding hands, chanting, and calling upon the elements and various deities, the activists claimed to be able to stop the war by making the Pentagon levitate several feet above the ground and purify it from evil energy. The performance not only attracted the intervention of the Army, but also the attention of national media. Employing performance for its ability to disrupt the expectations of the state regarding political protest proved to be an effective strategy for the activists, garnering widespread public support.

Countless contemporary examples point to the ability of performance to create unusual situations, mix art and political protest and mobilize bodies to take over public space. By highlighting the aesthetic elements of the everyday, or by introducing the spectacular in seemingly quotidian situations, performers often put into question the limits of what is accepted. New York-based group The Church of Stop Shopping and its leader, Reverend Billy, stage performances that target the symbols of consumerism and capitalism, such as Monsanto's headquarters or the Trump Tower on Manhattan's Fifth Avenue. Their performances bring together theatrical spectacle, street protest and religious sermons to draw attention to the economic and financial processes that are endangering the planet and creating poverty.

Giving the porous boundaries between artistic forms of performance and other social events, how do we define performance? From a performance studies perspective, a performance is defined by its *framing*. This means drawing certain spatial and temporal boundaries and looking at what happens within those boundaries *as* performance. In the previous example, we can set the frame at Reverend Billy's sermons and the Choir's responses and songs and analyse them as performance. But we might also want to choose a broader frame by including the audiences that the performance appeals to. Thus, we might want to include the pedestrians that stop to watch, those who pass by without looking, the security staff at Monsanto's headquarters, or the police patrols in front of Trump Tower. Doing so would yield a different definition of performance, with different participants and different stakes.

Social scientists, especially in the field of anthropology, have for a long time distinguished between cultural and social performances. *Cultural performances* are framed events with a beginning and an end, audiences and actors or performers, however broadly understood. Examples of cultural performance include plays, concerts, circus acts, storytelling, puppet shows, carnivals, parades and ritual ceremonies, such as weddings and funerals. Cultural performances are intentionally presented to an audience. *Social performances* are also communicative acts but they are not marked as specific events nor conducted in such a way that the people carrying them are aware of performing. They include everyday interactions of individuals, such as conversations, gestures, walking, eating, forms of greeting, etc. They are culturally specific behaviours that can include symbolic practices, but they are generally not framed as events presented to an audience. More recently, performance studies scholar Joshua Chambers-Letson has offered another useful distinction between quotidian and aesthetic performance. *Quotidian performances* are everyday acts of self-presentation, akin to what anthropologists have traditionally called social performances. *Aesthetic performances* are a step removed from the everyday and are meant to be encountered by audiences as aesthetic experiences, such as going to the theatre, the opera, a concert, or a performance art event.

Although establishing discrete categories for the study of performance can be quite useful as one first approaches performance studies as a field, it is important to remember that ultimately these categories are not set in stone. In framing something as a performance, distinctions between discrete categories often become blurry. Cultural performances can act as the gravitational centre that attracts and stimulates its own class of social performances, such as the interactions amongst those gathered in a theatre lobby before a play. Quotidian performances can be highly aesthetic, as people who cosplay know, and aesthetic performances can appear quite quotidian, or at least seek to intentionally blur the boundaries between the quotidian and the aesthetic with productive results, as seen in the examples of The Church of Stop Shopping and Hoffman's Pentagon exorcists. The following sections offer an overview of how performance is broadly understood and used in the field of performance studies.

PERFORMANCE IN EVERYDAY LIFE

In our daily interactions, we play different roles for different people in different settings. And although we always remain ourselves, different parts of us come to the fore in these roles. Hence, we might behave very differently at work, in church, while flirting with a love interest, or casually hanging out with a group of friends. Studying these everyday behaviours, Erving Goffman (1922–1982), a Canadian American sociologist, argued that all human activities that seek to influence others in any way, whether consciously or unconsciously, can be understood as performance. Goffman thought that by performing our *selves* in the everyday, we present a *front* to others, one that not only responds to what they expect of us, but also to the impressions we want to leave on them. Thus, things that might seem quite ordinary or even irrelevant can in fact be highly consequential, such as the way we dress, arrange our hair, talk, remain silent, gesticulate, walk and sit down. From this perspective, human interactions can be broken apart into their essential performance elements, such as actors, audiences, costumes, settings, or props. It is the relationship between these elements that allows us to extract meanings and cues on how to behave socially, even though much of this process happens unconsciously.

One of Goffman's essential contributions was the idea that when performing one's everyday self, someone might travel from belief to disbelief in what they are doing and vice versa. Thus, they might start performing with certain scepticism, only for the sake of their audience, but eventually end up feeling that their performance expresses some part of their authentic self. This idea resembles that longstanding piece of common wisdom that when we do something for long enough, it becomes an essential part of who we are. But the opposite is also true, in that we might repeat a certain behaviour and at some point start feeling increasingly estranged from it, as if we were forcing ourselves to do something that does not quite feel authentic. We will return to and expand upon this relationship between identity and the repetition of behaviour later when we talk about *performativity*.

Our everyday performances also mark our belonging to different communities, our beliefs and our values. They convey substantial information about who we are and who we want to be. Because we consciously or unconsciously mark our alignment with or our distance from particular communities and social groups, our performances might not always comply with social expectations. Sometimes, we might want to present ourselves in ways that specifically disrupt these, like a goth teenager craving forms of self-expression that veer away from the desires of their conservative parents. Other times, our performances of self simply cannot be contained within a particular set of expectations, or they might make us stand out in uncomfortable ways. We might not always be able to choose the ways we perform our gender, sexuality, race, or class, and this might determine the ways our performances – and by extension ourselves – are perceived in various social situations.

But whether we use our everyday performances to stand out, blend in, or hide in plain sight, whether we succeed or fail at what we are trying to convey when we perform, what seems clear is that there is no such thing as coming before others without performing. Crucially, these forms of everyday quotidian performance do not have to be consciously understood or defined as performance by their actors. Insofar as they have a presentational, communicative purpose in a given social setting, they can be analysed as such.

RITUALS

Social scientists have long noticed that in all cultures performance is an essential part of the social human experience and is deployed in rituals that mark important life transitions, heal the social fabric after moments of crisis, or solidify a sense of community with shared values and traditions. Anthropologists have traditionally divided rituals into two categories: sacred and secular. Sacred rituals are those related to religious or spiritual beliefs and generally involve some form of communication with the supernatural. Secular rituals are those related to the many facets of public and everyday life, such as state ceremonies or sport events. However, in many non-Western societies, and often also in Western society, the differences between sacred and secular rituals are blurred and we might see events that contain elements of both. For example, funerals held for soldiers killed while on military duty often involve both religious and public rituals. In many countries, including some in which religious and political life are supposedly separated, when an elected president or prime minister starts public duty, they take an oath on a Bible or other religious text. Whether sacred, secular, or mixed, all rituals are structured, usually collective events in which people engage in actions that feel important and transformative to them or their community. Usually, rituals involve clear divisions of roles and rules of participation. These roles and rules determine what actions each participant will perform. During rituals, people perform particular gestures, actions, speeches, songs, dances, etc. Performance is an essential part of ritual because the behaviours in which participants engage are repeated over time, often through generations, and are passed from body to body in a learning process that is embodied and physical.

In the 1960s, he was not American anthropologist Victor Turner (1920–1983) posited that ritual performance is used as an instrument to conjure up and create collective meaning, have transformative experiences, solidify communal life and beliefs, or recall a mythic past. He called the experience of togetherness that happens in rituals *communitas*, arguing that however transient or bound to the time and place of the ritual, the experience of togetherness momentarily abolishes the differences in status between the members of the community. *Communitas* has the temporary ability to bring people together as equals who share a common experience. We can see Turner's notion of *communitas* at work in any contemporary example of ritual. Sport fans wear their team's colours and attend games where they might perform particular chants, songs, or gestures that mark them as part of a collective. The attendants of a Catholic Eucharist ingest the holy wafer, and through this action build a sense of being one community in Christ. In the United States, the recital of the Pledge of Allegiance to begin congressional sessions, local government meetings, and in schools is a performance that solidifies the idea of nationhood. Across college campuses, fraternities and sororities perform rituals that mark their members as parts of a community.

The persistence of rituals in human societies across different times and geographical locations suggests that our species has always used performance to create and maintain community, to make sense of life transitions and difficult experiences, or to feel connected with supernatural or spiritual dimensions. Broadly speaking, in rituals, humans use performance to give meaning to their lives. Given the importance of rituals, it is not surprising that some people might feel very strongly about the 'right' ways of performing certain rituals, or have the impression that rituals are immutable and fixed over time. As with any other kind of performance, however, rituals can and do change. Often, new rituals are invented to promote or consolidate certain collective values. Sometimes, old rituals performed over long periods of time might change almost imperceptibly through the small differences that repetition entails. Finally, we might choose to change the way we perform a certain ritual to make a point about the status quo that the ritual upholds or represents. When some NFL players started to kneel in 2016 during the American national anthem to protest systemic racism in their country, they were deliberately changing their performance in a collective ritual of nationhood. In doing so, they used performance to call attention to the fact that the nation is not a neutral category but one that serves the interests of some individuals over others based on their race and class.

PERFORMATIVITY

In the 1960s, British philosopher J. L. Austin (1911–1960) developed his idea that language does more than just describe reality, and that some utterances or 'speech acts' have material and tangible consequences. He grouped these speech acts that do something in the world in a category that he labelled *performative*. He also argued that performative speech acts are different from *constative* speech acts, which merely describe the world. Austin also noticed that in order for speech acts to have their performative effect, specific social conventions have to be fulfilled. In one of his classic examples, the utterance 'I do' pronounced during a marriage ceremony has the power of binding two individuals in a social contract, but only in specific social circumstances. Some of these circumstances include that the words are pronounced by someone authorized to officiate the wedding, in front of witnesses, and provided that – at least at the time of his writing – the married individuals are a man and woman. Austin's essential contribution was to help us see that language *makes* the world as much as it describes it.

One of Austin's students, American philosopher John R. Searle (b. 1932), took Austin's definition of the performative a step further, arguing that performative language is not only circumscribed to special occasions. For Searle, all language can be performative when spoken with intention. And given that some sort of intention is almost always present in all utterances, Searle concluded that all language was performative.

Also drawing on Austin's theories, French philosopher Jacques Derrida (1930–2004) theorized that the effectiveness of speech in creating a particular reality is not so much related to the fulfilment of a set of circumstances that will give the utterance social validity, but to its iterability, that is, its repetition. Essential to Derrida's contribution is the idea that individual human intention in uttering something is highly determined by the structure of repetition of language. That is, the things we say mean something precisely because we share a set of conventions about their meaning with the people that we speak to, and these conventions about their meaning have been established through repetition. Returning to Austin's by way of Derrida shows us that uttering the words 'I do' in a marriage ceremony is socially binding not only because the occasion fulfils all the right requirements, but because marriage ceremonies have been repeated in more or less the same way for a very long time. Repetition is what gives performative speech its capacity to shape the world. Derrida's contribution shows that, when we utter performative speech acts, we do not simply get to make the world as if we had complete agency, but we insert ourselves in a process in which meanings are socially constructed in particular ways.

Contemporary feminist and queer theorist Judith Butler draws on Derrida's idea of language as iteration to argue that subjects' identities are produced by speech and that this production happens in social circumstances over which they do not have total control. In her book *Bodies that Matter*, published in 1993, Butler poses her theory of gender performativity as an example of how discourse produces bodies. Butler argues that gender is an enactment, one that responds to social expectations that are imposed on the individual from the very moment of birth. Nowadays, the performative dimension of gender might not strike many of us as shocking. We know that when adults dress girls in pink and boys in blue, encourage them to play with dolls or trucks, tell girls to be caring of others' feelings and boys to not cry 'like girls', they are in fact teaching children the notion that there are proper ways of being male or female. We also know that society has plenty of subtle and not so subtle ways of punishing those who do not ascribe to normative gender behaviours, or in different words, those who do not *perform* their gender quite like social customs prescribe – from bullying high school classmates to jail or the death penalty in some societies. If some of these ideas are widespread today, it is in part thanks to the work of feminist and queer scholars like Butler, who made the invaluable contribution of putting into academic language, and therefore legitimizing, the idea that gender is not simply natural or biological, but socially constructed. We can, therefore, understand the performativity of gender as the socially constructed dimension of gender through the repetition of embodied acts.

Butler also points out that our gender performances are neither completely shaped by society nor completely autonomous. In other words, even though we naturalize our gender through repetition, this naturalization is often incomplete and open to being contested. One does not just possess a gender, but more exactly one performs gender on a spectrum. Gender can be also performed against social expectations. Sometimes subjects cannot help but fail at performing normative gender expectations. This inability to conform to the norm, or standing out, reveals both the constructed nature of gender norms and their limits. Crucially, insofar as it posits bodies as both produced by and in tension with cultural norms, Butler's work on the performativity of gender offers an insight into other performative dimensions of identity and their relationship with social belonging, such as race, ethnicity, or class.

THE ANTI-PERFORMANCE PREJUDICE

At this point, the reader might rightfully wonder: is all human behaviour, both individual and social, a form of performance? If we are always performing, is there an authentic self, an essence of who we are as individuals that just *is*, without the compulsion to perform? These concerns are legitimate, but they are not entirely innocent since in their very framing, they situate performance and truth as polar opposites. We will break this assumption apart and analyse why it might be limiting to understand performance in this way. One of the goals of this book is to insist on a more nuanced definition of performance as always having some effect in the world. This is why the field of performance studies is crucially concerned with what performance *does*, even more so than what performance *is*.

A longstanding belief, especially in Western culture, equates performance with make-believe, and performing with pretending. The implication here is that something that is performed must necessarily not be entirely real, or respond to duplicitous intention. After all, when actors embody characters, they pretend to be people living in circumstances that have little to do with their own life. A performer can play a scientist, a cop, a queen, or a sex worker on screen or stage, and then change out of costume at the end of the day and return to a life devoid of the troubles that these characters face. In everyday life, we might occasionally refer to this or that person as *playing* a character, implying that they are purposefully insincere and pretending to be someone they are not. These notions of performances as fabrications that are opposed to the supposedly true essence of things are deeply embedded in our collective psyche. Why do we equate performance with deceit?

Associating performance with lie is an old and deep-seated prejudice. We can find the early evidence of it in Ancient Greece, where around 380 BC Plato denounced theatre as harmful to the political life of a healthy society. His concerns had to do with his philosophical approach to truth and reality. For Plato, anything that exists and that we can perceive through our senses is merely a reflection of a perfect universal truth, a copy of it. Thus, a table is a copy of the universal concept of table, already once removed from truth. In this logic, a theatrical performance is a copy of life, and since life itself is a copy of true reality, a performance is a copy of a copy. Performance, therefore, is in its very nature untrustworthy. Plato was also concerned with theatre's ability to present undesirable behaviours that spectators might feel inclined to copy, and with the dangers of performers imitating 'lesser' people, such as women and slaves.

The underlying suspicion that performance stands in opposition to truth has fuelled arguments against performance in different historical moments, from early Christianity to the Puritan movement. Anti-performance prejudice has not disappeared in contemporary times. In fact, it is not difficult to see Plato's anti-theatrical bias lurking in some contemporary public debates. Think how performing gets associated with moral corruption and political populism when we hear that certain candidates for office use their showmanship to attract votes, as if performing and deceiving were the same thing. A more accurate view of the matter, however, would beg us to consider that all political campaigns are performances in which different performance elements (costume, speech, gestures, props, etc.) are deployed to convey particular messages to particular target audiences. From this perspective, it is not performance that is the problem, but the ultimate goals for which performance is mobilized.

In essence, Plato's notion of performance was that of *mimesis*, the Greek word for imitation. Understanding performance as mimesis is not wrong. All animals, humans included, learn to survive and thrive in their natural environments by imitating others, thus re-performing behaviour that we see others perform. Imitation and repetition are critical parts of our learning processes, of how knowledge travels from one body to another. But reducing performance to its mimetic function is a very limited understanding of what performance is and the role it has in human life. When we perform, we do not merely imitate behaviour, but we also transform it, adapt it, and create it anew. When we perform, there is simply no repetition without difference. In this sense, we could say that performance *makes* the world as much as it imitates it.

NOT ONLY BODIES PERFORM

Despite our focus on the body as the essential instrument of performance, not all performances happen in and through bodies, or at least not exclusively. Our online performances of self might often reflect who we are offline, but they also take on a life of their own that exceeds the tangible reality of our embodied everyday selves. If Goffman were writing today, he would likely notice that our social media and communication technologies have exacerbated our need to perform ourselves for our audience, perhaps making us more self-aware of the gaze of others and the impressions we want to foreground. But he would also note that these technological advances have multiplied our available resources to curate our identities. From carefully crafted Instagram posts, where one's life is embellished, to the most extreme cases of catfishing, in which one might fabricate a completely fake identity to intentionally deceive others, online performances of self happen on a spectrum between the virtual and the actual. In addition, our daily interactions with technology go well beyond our conscious and voluntary presence online. When we browse different websites, read the news, communicate, make purchases, drive the car, or monitor our heart rate and speed during a run in the park, we generate bits of information and digital data that are captured and processed for different purposes by a wide range of corporate entities. This data tends to elude our awareness of how we perform ourselves and suggests that we might in fact have a vastly wider audience than we readily imagine. We could consider our digital data repositories to be disembodied performances of us that circulate in the world with different effects and consequences.

Performance also happens through technological forms meant to preserve and archive live forms of embodiment, such as video and photography. These and other archiving tools and practices not only have a documentary purpose but a life of their own, prompting us to reconsider the place of the body as the central instrument of performance. We know that regardless of how advanced recording technology might be, archived performances are not merely copies of the live performances they capture. As spectators, participants, or co-performers, our perceptual and emotional experience of a performance tends to be very different when we experience it live or mediated through recordings. This is not an argument that favours liveness, dismissing archived performances as secondary – although the debate on whether performance can be preserved or whether it is meant to disappear has been important in the field of performance studies – but is instead an invitation to consider the live and the archived as distinct but ultimately intertwined forms in which performance circulates.

Performance studies scholar Diana Taylor offers important insights into the constant interaction of archived and live forms of performance, or repertoire. The *repertoire* is composed of embodied acts that require the presence of participants to transmit culturally shared meanings and knowledge. The *archive*, on the other hand, is composed of those things that seem fixed and unchangeable, such as material remains, books, archaeological artefacts, etc. Although the former seems ephemeral and the latter durable, Taylor undoes this assumption by arguing that both offer different performances. Archives are never stable, but are animated by selection processes, curatorial endeavours and interpretative explanations projected onto the past to make it intelligible. Though apparently ephemeral, repertoires in fact show an extraordinary ability to survive, transmitted through generations as embodied knowledge, often persisting despite active attempts to suppress them. Even as it is re-performed, and therefore transformed and adapted, the repertoire is stored in the body. For Taylor, the body itself is a medium for performance, one amongst many others. As a medium, the body stores behaviours that are learned, shared and transmittable.

Even though in performance art the body is the central element of the artistic practice, a significant part of this genre also incorporates other media. In these works, performance exceeds the physical presence of the performers, deriving its significance from the interplay amongst all the media employed. For instance, in their ongoing collaboration under the name Disorientalism, Asian American artists Katherine Behar and Marianne M. Kim combine live performance, video art, installations and photography to explore the effects of technologized labour, junk culture and capitalism. In *TV Maintenance*, the performers seemed trapped behind the glass screen of a giant TV, performing labours of maintenance such as cleaning and wiping. In turn, this performance is presented to spectators as four short videos, each of the duration of a TV commercial. Spectators walk around a gallery-like space, being able to choose the order in which they will watch the four commercials. The performers' bodies, the screen they clean, the video commercials, and the small screens in which spectators access them all constitute different layers of mediation through which a performance that comments on contemporary labour regimes happens.

Finally, outside of the genre of performance art, there are other forms of contemporary performance that would be unthinkable without the interplay of digital media and embodied action. For instance, whereas digital media activism has been considered secondary to physical forms of protest, as if its main roles were to merely document and circulate activist performances that happen on the street, performance studies scholar Marcela Fuentes debunks this view. Studying contemporary forms of performing protest in Latin America, Fuentes demonstrates there is a cooperative relationship between digital media and embodiment, which she refers to as 'performance constellations'. These are hybrid, networked and decentred combinations of bodies and media technologies mobilized to achieve specific political goals. When students protesting the privatization of public education in Chile in 2011 organized a zombie flash mob, the success of their action was in great part due to their organizing simultaneously live and online.

All of the examples Fuentes examines encourage us to consider the ways in which embodied performance not only travels through channels other than bodies, but in fact is shaped and transformed by its symbiotic relationship with technologies and archiving practices.

WHAT IS PERFORMANCE STUDIES?

Performance studies is an interdisciplinary field of research that combines theory and practice to examine performance as an essential element of human life and society, from performance art, theatrical spectacle, dance, music, circus, carnivals, festivals, parades and expressive movement, to all kinds of sacred and secular rituals and ceremonies, everyday life performances and the performative elements of identity, such as gender, race and sexuality. All forms of human action with communicative purpose, whether conscious or unconscious, could be considered performance and therefore be included as topics to research in performance studies. Scholars and practitioners in performance studies not only study performances as staged practices and aesthetic objects, but also as expressions of broader cultural and social processes. The field's investment in studying cultural and social phenomena as processes rather than fixed objects entails that the conceptual categories it uses to do so, such as performance and performativity, are bound to perpetually change and expand. Performance studies scholar Richard Schechner illuminates this tendency of the field by asserting that even though not everything *is* performance, everything can be studied *as* performance. This assertion signals that performance studies is far less concerned with what performance is than what it does, or the functions performance has in social life. In other words, if an embodied cultural expression has social significance, it can be considered *as* performance.

At its core, the field of performance studies focuses on the body as an agent of knowledge production and transmission, complementing other academic fields that have traditionally privileged text or media as objects of study. This does not mean that the field excludes the study of texts, images, film, or other objects, but rather that it always interrogates these objects' relationship to the body and its social life.

In this sense, one of the field's radical contributions is to assert that bodies produce knowledge, and therefore need to be taken as seriously as texts, documents and others forms of data, both in academia and in public life. Because bodies are not abstract entities but are concrete material realities that condition how people are perceived, as well as how they interact and move through the world according to their race, gender, sexuality, class, size, ability, etc. – in other words, because bodies exist in a social structure shaped by power – the field of performance studies also examines and critiques existing power arrangements and forms of oppression, and points to the conditions that would make a better world possible.

The focus on the body as an object of study implies that the field of performance studies is also implicitly concerned with the study of diverse life experiences and their differences. This view questions universalism – the idea that human experiences are the same regardless of cultural differences – in favour of more nuanced understandings of how different identities are shaped by power and are placed in hierarchical relationships to each other. For instance, we know that despite biological differences, masculinity and femininity are not natural categories, but are in fact historically and socially constructed as polar opposites. In patriarchal societies, this division, alongside the erasure of other gender identities that do not conform with either of the two, upholds a power hierarchy in which the masculine is often equated with strength and the feminine with fragility or weakness. Both categories are constituted in opposition to each other. To give another example, the history of Western European colonization in Africa and the subsequent transatlantic slave trade created the racial categories of whiteness and blackness as polar opposites. Whiteness was equated with civilization and rationality, while blackness with irrationality and wildness. Contemporary notions of gender and race – and identity more broadly – are neither neutral nor natural, but come from specific histories of power and domination and cannot be understood in isolation from each other. Starting from this essential premise, the field of performance studies is concerned with how performance shapes different life experiences and identities and how performance might help disrupt histories of oppression and contribute to building more egalitarian societies. In this sense, performance studies questions the prevalence of Western culture, values and economic models, their role in structures of oppression, and their ongoing dominance in contemporary global society.

Because of its critical view of the distribution of power in society, the field of performance studies employs a research methodology in which performance is at the same time *event*, *theory* and *method*. This means that performance studies examines performances as framed events, uses performance theory as the foundation to understand how meaning is socially created and transmitted through the body, and employs performance as a methodology of research, by both studying life phenomena as performance and creating performances to intervene in social processes. As a consequence of this triple understanding of performance, the field tends to blur the boundaries between scholar, artist and activist.

PERFORMANCE ETHNOGRAPHY AND PRACTICE

This chapter has so far discussed how performance constitutes the world, but performance studies is also vitally concerned with how performance can be used to gain critical insights into the functioning of the world and transform it. Because bodies harbour cultural knowledge and transmit it, the study of embodied behaviour through ethnographic methods is an important part of the field of performance studies. This also includes the adaptation of ethnographic data to staged performances.

Ethnography has been long used by social scientists to study human groups in their cultural specificities. Much of this tradition, however, has considered the researcher to be an outsider who can observe and report the behaviour of the subjects they examine from an objective point of view. Performance ethnography has added to this tradition by presenting a more complex and accurate perspective on the role of the researcher and their relationship with the community they study. While social science ethnographic methods presume this is a neutral relationship, performance ethnography starts from the premise that such neutrality has never existed because people inhabit the world embedded in political narratives and value judgments about their identities. Performance studies scholar Dwight Conquergood (1949–2004), who studied Hmong refugees in Thailand and gang members in Chicago, among other communities, developed the idea that studying social groups is akin to a dialogue between the researcher and the people they study. Instead of observing behaviour from a removed perspective, Conquergood thought that ethnographers always *coperform* with their interlocutors, and that both parties are transformed in this performance. The very presence of a researcher might modify the way individuals in a social group choose to perform themselves. Ethnographers and their interlocutors might also have to negotiate power differences such as class, status, race, or access to resources and knowledge, among others. Cultural differences, disparate worldviews and divergent sensibilities can also separate the ethnographer and the social group they study, but can also serve as an opportunity for everybody involved to learn and be transformed in the exchange.

Whereas traditionally, the results of ethnographic research in the social sciences have been presented in writing, performance studies has strived to incorporate staged performances as not only a legitimate mode of presenting research, but in fact as a mode that might be better suited than writing to transmit the often subtle but resilient social threads that bind societies together. Thus, the performances that happen in the field between researcher and interlocutors can be communicated as performance themselves. D. Soyini Madison calls these 'performed ethnography'. In staging ethnographic research, performance studies scholars/practitioners might choose to include other things that paint a complex picture of a local site and the human groups that they study. Music, sound, image, legal documents, literary texts, news headlines, personal diaries, letters, or emails, etc. alongside with data from the field compiled in different media, from written field notes, interviews, photography and video. Then, these materials might be combined with staged live performance to create performed ethnographies. Performed ethnography is animated by the need to bring an experience to audiences, one that appeals to more than delivering information and content. Performance, in all its sensorial and symbolic richness, is more akin to how we experience the world through our multiple senses than writing can be. From the perspective of performed ethnography, embodied practices enrich theory and open up multiple ways of creating and sharing knowledge.

WHY PERFORMANCE?

Because of the arguably ambitious scope of the field, in which performance eludes a fixed definition, performance studies has been traditionally criticized for not having a specific object of study. In other words, if anything can be performance, then nothing is performance, or so the argument goes. One might respond, however, that scientists have been arguing for a long time that the entirety of matter is made of atoms and nobody questions chemistry or physics on the basis that if everything is atoms, then nothing is. Just in the same way that our understanding of the physical world improved greatly when we learned that all matter is made of particles that are invisible to us and that interact with each other, our understanding of social life also expands considerably once we start looking at human behaviour through the lens of performance. Performance lies at the very essence of how our bodies interact with others and the world around us. Because humans are social beings, we tend to see the world and explain it through notions and concepts whose meanings we create collectively. Even more importantly, the ways we see and make sense of the world relate directly with the ways we inhabit it. And it so happens that the processes through which we collectively create and communicate meanings are, in fact, performances. As a species, humans make themselves and their world through performance. This does not mean that we have complete control over all our performances and their consequences, but we are certainly far from powerless. Perhaps here lies the greatest potential in understanding our social worlds through performance: if we create our own realities, then the worlds we envision might be within our reach once we start performing them.

FURTHER READING/RESEARCH

Watch some of the interviews included in the 'What is Performance Studies? Interview Series' on the Hemispheric Institute website at hemisphericinstitute. org/en/hidvl/hidvl-int-wips.html

2

PERFORMANCE ART

WHAT IS PERFORMANCE ART?

Performance art is a genre of artistic expression that emerged in the 1960s and 1970s, initially amongst a relatively young generation of artists working in the United States, Europe and Japan who were concerned with transgressing the boundaries of traditional art domains. With influences from a wide array of artistic practices such as painting, sculpture, film–making, dance and theatre, these artists often labelled their work as *body art*, *action art*, *live art* or *conceptual art*. In fact, the term *performance art* only started to be widely used some time later, in the 1970s and 1980s. What these early performance artists had in common was using their own bodies as their medium of expression and seeking to disrupt the role of audiences as passive intellectual observers of an artwork. Yoko Ono's 'Cut Piece' illustrates these characteristics. First performed in Kyoto and Tokyo in the summer of 1964 and then at Carnegie Hall in New York City in March 1965, in this piece Yoko Ono (b.1933) sat kneeling on stage, dressed, with scissors placed in front of her, and invited audience members to approach and cut pieces of clothes off her body. While Ono prompted spectators to choose what they wanted to take from her performance in quite a literal way, her piece made explicit something that is true of all performance art, that audiences play a significant and active role in giving meaning to the work.

Although an exhaustive history of performance art is beyond the scope of the present book, this chapter will chart some canonical performance artists and tendencies of the genre, as well as briefly

DOI: 10.4324/9780429286377-3

discuss its history. Unlike more traditional theatrical performance, in performance art there is no character clearly marked as different from the actor who embodies it. Rather, the performer's actions are understood as an extension of themselves, a sort of public persona, which places the audience in a direct relationship with the performer. The audience's reception of the performance is thus deeply marked by their understanding of the performer's identity, which in turn elicits questions about the very processes through which identities are formed and understood in society. In fact, we could say that among all art forms, performance art is *par excellence* concerned with the relational aspects of identity, that is, how different identities exist in relation to each other. This is precisely one of the main reasons that performance art constitutes such a significant turn in cultural history, as we will see in the next few sections.

It is not a coincidence that the history of performance art runs in parallel with the history of social movements and upheavals starting in the late 1960s that questioned the status quo and expanded the rights of minorities, such as second wave feminism, black and women of colour feminism, movements for gay rights, the Civil Rights and anti-war movements in the United States, and student movements in Europe and Latin America. Beyond their specific political agendas, what all these movements achieved was to start breaking apart a notion of subjectivity that had been deeply settled in the Western imaginary and according to which the body is a self-contained, coherent unity that contains our essence as individuals. These movements started to demonstrate that categories such as gender, race and sexuality are in fact not timeless and immutable, but the result of long histories of power differences amongst groups of people. These social and historical changes also coincide with changes in the philosophical conception of the self. As mentioned in the performativity sections of the previous chapter, the work of authors such as J. L. Austin, Erving Goffman, Jacques Derrida and later Judith Butler helped reframe identity from a fixed feature to a performative endeavour inherently embedded in social context and relationships. Against this political, social and philosophical background, performance art emerged as a genre that allowed artists and audiences to explore the histories through which identities are formed and their contemporary ramifications.

THE ORIGINS OF PERFORMANCE ART

Some scholars of performance date the origins of performance art much earlier than the 1960s and 1970s, and build a continuous history in which performance art is the culmination of a series of boundary-breaking artistic practices focused on the body as both the subject and object of art. This view is represented, for instance, by performance art historian RoseLee Goldberg (b. 1947), who in her book *Performance Art: From Futurism to the Present* outlines the similarities between performance art as it emerged in the 1960s and avant-garde art genres from the early twentieth century, such as futurism, Dada and surrealist performance. For example, Goldberg mentions that the evenings at the infamous Cabaret Voltaire, a night club funded in Zurich, Switzerland in 1916, where avant-garde European artists of that time gathered for poetry recitals, live painting or musical improvisations, constitute an incipient form of performance art events. A couple of decades later, exiled European artists who moved to the United States during the 1930s to escape fascism took their avant-garde experiments to New York, influencing American artists in the following decades. American composer John Cage (1912–1992) is considered one of the artists who was influenced by the arrival of this avant-garde lineage in the United States. Cage is often cited as having organized the first *happening* in 1952 while teaching at Black Mountain College in North Carolina. Cage's happening at Black Mountain College was a multi-media performance event that included, among other participants, experimental choreographer and dancer Merce Cunningham (1919–2009), known for his 'site-specific' choreographic works. Site-specific performance are pieces created with a particular place in mind and the meaning of which is heavily informed by the characteristics of that location.

Another often cited precursor of performance art is American painter Jackson Pollock (1912–1956), who shifted the orientation of his huge canvases from vertical to horizontal and created his paintings using new techniques, such as dripping paint on the canvas from above. By employing massive canvases in this way, Pollock transformed the process of painting into events that included movement, action and the use of different materials. In these events, his body was as essential to the final product as his brushes or his canvas. In the 1960s, this tendency to foreground the body of artists as well as the process of art-making itself shifted the focus from the result, that is, the painting as a final object, to the *embodied* process of painting. Allan Kaprow (1927–2006), a seminal figure in this history for coining the term 'happening', cited Pollock as one of his major inspirations. Kaprow had started his art career as a painter and art history scholar and studied composition with John Cage at The New School before replacing painting for happenings in the late 1950s. Happenings mixed together theatrical performance and art exhibit and became popular in the New York City art scene. Taking place in lofts, small art galleries or on the street, and gathering small audiences of a few dozen people, happenings were meant to be non-replicable, unique events in which viewers engaged art as an immersive participatory experience. The Living Theatre and the Judson Dance Theatre, both based in New York City, were two performance groups that were essential in the early experimentation with happenings. Both were experimental collectives concerned with taking theatre out of traditional settings and into the streets, and who sought to collapse the differences between staged performance and everyday live action. The Judson Dance Theatre, in fact, was a collective of artists working in different media, such as film, dance, music, painting and writing, who engaged in interdisciplinary collaboration. Another important exponent of early performance art was the international artist group Fluxus, which included artists from the United States, Europe and Japan who were organized in a structure of loose affiliation often based on friendships. Fluxus members collaborated in art events and festivals held across the three continents in the 1960s. Even more interdisciplinary than the Judson Dance Theatre, Fluxus included dancers, musicians, poets, architects, designers, writers, publicists and printers who sought to push the boundaries of art disciplines and created experimental work.

Goldberg's historical account starting with avant-garde art in the early twentieth century suggests that the foundations for what would later coalesce into performance art had been built across different experimental art practices and media for decades. However, there are also scholars of performance who question this view of a seemingly smooth history of artistic transgression culminating in the birth of performance art in the 1960s. Performance art historian Amelia Jones holds this latter position. Jones does not deny the influences of avant-garde and experimental artists and movements in the emergence of performance art or 'body art' in the 1960s and 1970s, but argues that the latter constitutes more of a rupture than a continuity with some principles that had been foundational to Western art history. In her book *Body Art: Performing the Subject*, Jones points out that the most significant change brought about by performance art was destabilizing the conception of the subject that had been essential to European modernism. This means that, in contrast to the modernist understanding of the body as a vessel for a person's consciousness and identity, starting in the 1960s, identity and self have become increasingly understood as performative processes of which the body is a fundamental part. Performance art, then, becomes a uniquely positioned art form to reflect this change. With its focus on the body and its creation of meaning through the open-ended relationship between artists and spectators, performance art shows us that identities and subjectivities are always in construction and are situated in a person's particular circumstances rather than universally applicable to everyone. Performance art ties identity to the material body and its differences, rather than abstract notions of the human.

Jones also argues that performance art emerged at a time in which ways of understanding the role of the artist were starting to change in the art world. While for most of Western art history the artist remained invisible to the spectator, letting their oeuvre speak for itself, in performance art the body of the artist takes centre stage. This is no small thing, because as performance art demonstrated, remaining invisible had been a privilege only afforded to white male artists, whose artistic genius was supposedly transcendent, divorced from their embodied daily experience and able to speak of universal human preoccupations. Performance artists of colour, women artists and queer and non-binary artists have not usually had the privilege of being understood as speaking abstractly for and to all humankind. When allowed to participate in institutional art circuits at all, their art tends to be received by spectators as a direct representation of their experience as members of a particular minority. Foregrounding the body of the artist in performance, then, was for many artists belonging to minority groups both a response to these issues and a rupture with notions of disembodied artistic genius in Western art history.

To be sure, it is not that people belonging to minorities only started to be visible in art and performance in the 1960s and 1970s. Throughout art history, white artists had represented people of colour in their work, but had done so in ways that were overtly or inherently racist. In performance, Euro-American colonial history comes with a centuries-long, debasing tradition of exhibiting bodies of racial, gender or disabled minorities in circuses, freakshows or world fairs. And even within this history, the people exhibited did not stand passive but often engaged in subtle forms of resistance and agency against the ways they were being represented. What was different starting in the 1960s and 1970s is that the cultural landscape was ripe for the proliferation of subjects belonging to minority groups to exhibit artistic work in which they could appear in their own terms. Their work staged their bodies in relationship to audiences in ways that questioned the very ways in which we ascribe bodies to certain categories such as feminine, gay, black, indigenous, disabled, etc. The staging of the body in these terms in performance art seeks to unsettle spectators' relationship with and participation in the very processes of meaning through which bodies are seen and understood.

To sum up, performance art emerged in the 1960s and 1970s, borrowed from boundary-breaking experimental impulses that had been part of the art world in prior decades, and reflected radical shifts in the ways identity and subjectivity were understood and talked about in society. In the following sections we will delve into some examples of performance art, dwelling particularly on feminist and queer performance, as well as performance by black, indigenous and people of colour performers. This history also reveals one of the essential tensions of performance art: While it could be described as a Western art genre because it emerged and developed primarily in the United States and Europe – in addition to Japan – the history of performance art is largely made by artists working from minoritarian positions of race, gender and sexuality to decentre the very foundations of Western civilization as a white supremacist, heterosexual and patriarchal system.

FEMINIST PERFORMANCE ART

Feminist performance art seeks to address and politicize women's issues in relationship to sexism and patriarchal structures that oppress women. Needless to say, not all performance art created by women is feminist, and not all women performance artists might define their work as feminist performance even when it deals with issues affecting women. Amongst all the works that could be labelled as feminist performance art we find a considerable variety of perspectives. This variety responds to the diversity that characterizes feminist movements, their historical evolution and their internal debates and tensions. What seems certain is that one cannot recount the history of performance art without addressing feminism and the influence that the political struggle of sexual and gender minorities has had in art and performance practices over the past decades.

As described in the last section, the 1960s experimental art scene was ripe for interdisciplinary collaboration between artists, formal experimentation and direct audience participation. Many of the artists working at that time were interested in art as a social process rather than a final result. This presented an interesting paradox for many women artists: while, as artists, they found fertile ground for creative experimentation in the early 1960s art scene, as women, they also found a lot of deeply entrenched sexism. They not only had a harder time than their male colleagues accessing circuits of art exhibition, but their work was also received with harsher critiques, or directly dismissed, even when they created experimental work that was similar in content to that of their male counterparts. The art scene was even tougher for women of colour performers, often forgotten in the canonical history of early feminist performance art, with a few exceptions such as Yoko Ono or Shigeko Kubota (1937–2015). Women performance artists concerned with asserting their individuality as artists in the 1960s soon realized that, in order to talk about women's experiences, they had to push the boundaries of what was considered to be fit subjects of art, and that doing so was an inherently feminist issue. Unsurprisingly, the art world, which had always made room for women to be muses to male artists and sexual objects for male gaze consumption, was not as open for women artists who wanted to talk about their experiences from a gender perspective. Even those women performance artists who did not readily identify as feminist had to contend with the fact that pervasive sexism conditioned how they, their bodies and their creative work were perceived. This is why it could be argued that, though not all performance art created by women is intentionally feminist, all performance art created by women invariably brings up questions related to how women are perceived in society, and this is a feminist question.

The early work of Carolee Schneeman (1939–2019) reflects some of these issues. Schneeman was one of the pioneer women artists in the New York body art scene of the early 1960s. She participated in the social circles of artists involved in happenings, Fluxus and the Judson Dance Theatre. Her 1963 piece 'Eye Body: 36 Transformative Actions' reflects a lot of the experimental impulses of the time. In the piece, Schneeman created a whole environment in her loft for spectators to navigate in which they encountered broken glass and mirrors, motorized umbrellas, plastic sheets, photographs, large painted panels and the artist's naked body covered in grease, paint, chalk or slithering live snakes. While gesturing towards traditional spectatorial expectations of naked women in art as objects on display, Schneeman was also reclaiming the terms of her own representation. A year later, she created 'Meat Joy' (1964), which featured a group of male and female performers playfully rolling around, smearing their bodies in paint and playing with raw fish, chicken and sausage. Performed in Paris and London, 'Meat Joy' was a celebration of the sensual and sensorial dimensions of the physical body in line with 1960s ideas about the need to liberate the body from bourgeois moral constraints.

Fluxus member Shigeko Kubota (1937–2015) is another pioneer of body art. In 1965, Kubota performed her piece 'Vagina Painting' in New York. Echoing both Pollock and female anatomical functions, Kubota squatted down on a canvas and dripped red paint with a brush attached to her underwear. The piece was a direct comment of the presumption that women's art could only address women's issues but not universal human concerns. Alongside Yoko Ono's 'Cut Piece', Kubota's 'Vagina Painting' also constitutes an early work that questioned racialized assumptions of Japanese – and more broadly Asian – women as passive and docile subjects. Perhaps not surprisingly, many people in the art world, even within experimental circles such as Fluxus, found Ono's 'Cut Piece', Kubota's 'Vaginal Painting' and Schneeman's 'Eye Body' displeasing and in poor taste. The harsh criticism against these performances and the fact that male body artists making similarly explicit work were not so readily disparaged by critics suggests that despite the sexual revolutions of the 1960s, naked bodies and an unapologetic display of anatomical or sexual functions were considered much more distasteful when the artist was a woman.

To understand this double standard in the reception of women's work, one has to look at art history. As performance studies scholar

Rebecca Schneider has argued in her book *The Explicit Body in Performance*, female performance artists who were using their bodies in explicit ways starting in the 1960s unsettled gendered dynamics that had deep roots in art history. To be sure, it was not the display of their bodies that was shocking, as female bodies had always been depicted explicitly in art history. What was different about women body artists is that they were not displaying their bodies as objects of male work, but taking over the authority of representing themselves. Schneider believes that in explicitly displaying their bodies, these women artists were not altogether avoiding objectification and the long history of representing women as objects of desire rather than agents that actively desire. Rather, in being both an image to be contemplated and the makers of their own image, these female performance artists brought attention to these very complex issues of representation. Schneider also offers a very valuable insight into considerations of women performance artists' alleged narcissism. For the accusation that a woman exhibiting her naked body is an exhibitionist or a narcissist implicitly means that she can only be conceived of as object and not subject. Because she is seen as an object, her artwork cannot be anything but the object's exhibition, unlike her male counterparts, who even while appearing naked are given the consideration of an artist whose nudity is part of a broader artistic intention. In other words, a naked man could be considered an artistic genius experimenting with nudity, but a naked woman is an egocentric looking for attention.

The negative reception of body art pieces by women artists confirmed for many of them that in order to be accepted in the art world they needed to attack the underlying sexist assumptions that structured it. As a result, by the 1970s the feminist critique of the existing misogyny of the art world was much more explicit, and numerous women artists were making work under an overtly feminist label. Schneeman's 1975 piece 'Interior Scroll' is a good example of this evolution. While her early performances had been about asserting her individual position in the art world, in this piece Schneeman pulled a paper scroll out of her vagina and read a text that was a direct quotation of a male film maker's critique of her art as being excessively sensitive and focused on her personal feelings.

While in the 1960s the avant-garde centre of performance art had been New York City, in the 1970s a strong feminist performance art movement also emerged on the West Coast of the United States. In 1971, Judy Chicago (b. 1939) founded the first feminist art program in the Unites States at Fresno State College, later moving to teach at California Institute for the Arts. In both schools, feminist performance occupied an essential place in the curriculum and brought together a community of women artists who would influence each other for decades. Chicago was also one of the artists and scholars who founded Womenhouse, an abandoned mansion in Hollywood that was transformed into an experimental performance space for artists creating work that dealt with women's experiences, such as motherhood, menstruation, house work, domestic violence, sexual abuse, etc. Following the feminist axiom that 'the personal is political', Womenhouse constituted an exceptional space at a time when women experiences were dismissed as irrelevant art subjects. Chicago's infamous 'Menstruation Bathroom' was an installation in the bathroom of Womenhouse that included a trashcan full of pads and tampons soaking in menstrual blood and a counter that displayed products marketed for female consumption during their periods. While shocking for certain audiences, the installation was a critique of the sexism promoted by the advertising industry and society's taboo about menstrual blood. After leaving CalArts, Chicago became one of the founders of Women's Building, an independent arts education and exhibition space for women that was active from 1973 to 1992.

In the late 1970s, a vibrant feminist performance art scene coalesced around these art programs and spaces on the West Coast, influencing the work of many notable feminist artists. Suzanne Lacy (b. 1945), who had been one of Judy Chicago's former students, collaborated with Leslie Lebowitz in 1977 to protest the high incidence of rape in Los Angeles by organizing a series of performance events called 'Three Weeks in May'. The events included a fifty-foot map of Los Angeles placed in the vicinity of City Hall and onto which the artists recorded, with info provided by the Los Angeles Police Department, daily sexual assaults taking place in the city and their exact location. Other feminist groups, artists and activists participated in public meetings, performances and self-defence workshops around the city to discuss the pervasiveness of sexual assault and demand policies to protect women. The events also aimed to transcend the secrecy and shame associated with rape by having a public dialogue.

Part of this agenda was engaging the media to cover and speak about the performances in the hope of reaching a wider audience. 'Three Weeks in May' reflected Lacy's view that art can be successfully used as an instrument of public intervention on social issues.

Amidst the consolidation of feminist performance art in the 1970s, women of colour artists such as Ana Mendieta (1948–1985) and Adrian Piper (b. 1948) spoke out about the fact that much of the feminist performance art world comprised a white, middle class movement that excluded or overlooked women of colour's voices and experiences. Cuban-born and US-based Ana Mendieta used her performance artwork to explore the connection of femininity, spirituality and nature. In her *silueta* (Spanish for 'silhouette') series, Mendieta left imprints of her silhouette in mud or sand, painted her outline onto walls, or created her silhouette using a variety of materials such as twigs, leaves, flowers, blood or fire. Influenced by pre-Columbian religions and Afro-Caribbean spiritual practices such as Santería, Mendieta's performances also symbolized her search for identity as a form to connect with her lost Latin American heritage.

Starting as a conceptual artist in the 1960s, Adrian Piper's extremely prolific career has developed across diverse areas such as performance art, multi-media art practice and philosophy, and she became the first African American woman to receive tenure as a philosophy professor in the United States. In the 1970s, Piper developed a series of street performances called 'Catalysis' in which she altered her appearance and carried out everyday activities in public places to elicit the public's responses unmediated by the predetermined social codes of art exhibition spaces. In these performances, Piper sought to raise questions about how one's body and its racial and gender identity are perceived and given meaning through the gaze of others. In her 1986 piece 'My Calling Card #1', Piper handed out her card at dinner and cocktail parties to people who had made racist comments in her presence. The cards contained a brief text in which Piper brought to the attention of her interlocutor that they had made a racist remark, possibly after mistaking her light-skin complexion as white.

Mendieta and Piper were precursors of many other black, indigenous and women of colour performance artists who, starting in the 1980s, were using their work to explore how race, sexuality and identity intersect with gender. The work of these artists both reflected and fuelled the diversity of positions in feminist movements and enriched performance studies scholarship.

EXPANDING THE BOUNDARIES OF PERFORMANCE ART

Whereas in the 1970s feminist performance artists had to appeal to an essential idea of womanhood in a strategic attempt to counter the devaluation of women in the arts and bring women together under a common cause, in the 1980s feminist performance artists sought to interrogate this essentialism. They criticized early feminist artists for flattening identity differences under an essential image of 'woman' and started considering that gender intersects with other identity categories such as race, sexuality or class, producing a wide variety of personal experiences. They also started interrogating the very category of 'woman', turning their interest to critical theory, a field of study that understood gender itself as a form of performance and a social construct. In social theory, the 1980s and 1990s brought about the proliferation of works addressing interlocking forms of oppression. Fields of inquiry such as critical race studies, queer theory and women of colour feminism became well-defined academic disciplines and contributed ideas to public discourse. Not coincidentally, alongside this dialogue between art and social theory, performance studies became consolidated as an academic field, as we will see in the last chapter of this book.

Performance artists at this time were pushing the limits of the genre by calling attention to its limited diversity and explicitly seeking to foreground the experiences of sexual, gender, racial, ethnic and disabled minorities. They were also reflecting the political activism of the time, a subject we will cover more in depth in Chapter 5. In the United States, the 1980s AIDS epidemic and the particularly unresponsive public health policies towards it galvanized LGBT populations and their allies in an activist fight that changed both performance art and activism. At the same time, performance artists belonging to sexual and gender minorities became targets of right-wing politicians and organizations during the so-called 'culture wars'. The moral panic against performance artists culminated in the infamous case of the 'NEA Four' in 1990, when the chairman of the National Endowment for the Arts vetoed grants that had been allocated to Tim Miller, Holly

Hughes, Karen Finley and John Fleck in an initial evaluation by a peer review committee. Although the artists took the case to court and got their grants back in 1993, their case sparked heated debates about censorship in the arts and the hostility of conservative factions towards sexual and gender minorities, as three of the four artists were openly homosexual.

Although performance by Latino artists had strong precursors in the 1970s such as the ASCO group in Los Angeles and Ana Mendieta, the 1980s and 1990s saw a boom of Latino performance art both across Latin American countries and from Latino artists working in the United States. In Latin America, performance art had notable precursors in the mid-twentieth century with visual artists such as Lygia Clark (1920–88) and Raphael Montañez Ortiz (b.1934), as well as with non-object art practices in Mexico. However, it was in the 1980s that performance art as an artistic genre rose to prominence, becoming deeply political and seeking to contest social injustice and totalitarian political regimes. During the dictatorship of Augusto Pinochet in Chile, for example, CADA (Colectivo de Acciones de Arte, or Art Actions Collective) was a group formed by visual artists, writers, poets and academics who undertook artistic interventions in public space as a form of political dissent. In a series of actions grouped under the title 'Para No Morir de Hambre en el Arte' (Not to Die of Hunger in the Arts) in 1979, CADA distributed powdered milk among families living in a poor neighbourhood of Santiago, read a text about Chile's precarious economy in front of the United Nations building, and made an installation in an art gallery containing, among other things, milk left to discompose. 'Para No Morir' was a denunciation of the conditions of hunger and malnutrition affecting the poor in Chile. In their 'No +' action of 1983, they placed signs of 'no +' on walls around the city inviting anonymous citizens to complete the slogan with phrases such as 'no + dictatorship' and 'no + hunger'.

Within this rich tradition of political performance, the work of Guatemalan performance artist Regina José Galindo (b.1974) responds to the amnesia and erasure of the Guatemalan civil war and genocide. Starting her career in the 1990s, Galindo often enacts rituals of violence on her body, pointing to how violence has continued to target women and ethnic minorities even after the end of the dictatorship. In her 2003 piece '¿Quién puede borrar las huellas?' (Who can erase the traces?), Galindo walked between the building of the Congress of

Guatemala and the National Palace, stopping every few steps to dip her feet in a basin containing human blood. With this performance, she protested former dictator Ríos Montt's presidential candidacy in the country's democratic elections.

In 1992, many Latino performance artists whose work was prone to political commentary took advantage of the five hundredth anniversary of the Europeans' arrival to the Americas to make work that reflected on the power relations inherited from colonialism and how they continue to structure the contemporary world. In a highly humorous piece called 'Indigurrito' (a fusion of the words 'indigenous' and 'burrito'), Cuban American performance artist Nao Bustamante (b. 1969) transformed a burrito into a phallic symbol by strapping it to her crotch and invited white men in the audience to kneel in front of her and take a bite of it as a ritual of apology for five hundred years of oppression.

Performance artists Coco Fusco (b. 1960) and Guillermo Gómez-Peña (b. 1955) designed a travelling performance that they took to London, Madrid, Sidney, New York, and Washington, D.C., among other places. Fusco and Gómez-Peña embodied caged Amerindians from an imaginary island in the Gulf of Mexico that had allegedly remained undiscovered by the Europeans for five centuries. Remaining in the cage for three days at a time, they undertook 'traditional tasks' of their tribe such as sewing voodoo dolls, lifting weights or watching television. They were taken to the bathroom on leashes and fed by two guards who also served as interpreters between them and the audience. Their original intention was to create a satire of Western views of 'exotic' people and the centuries-long history of exhibiting colonized subjects for European audiences. To their surprise, and despite the satiric tone of the performance, many audience members on both sides of the Atlantic believed the fiction, addressing them as if they were 'savages'. Their travelling performance, compiled in a documentary called 'The Couple in the Cage' dramatized the ways in which colonialism still structures inter-cultural encounters between people in the present.

'The Couple in the Cage' echoed in certain ways an earlier performance by Native American artist James Luna (1950–2018), who in 'The Artifact Piece' (1987) had displayed his body in an exhibition case at the San Diego Museum of Man among some of the museum's collection of Native American artefacts and objects. With this work,

Luna offered a critical view of museums' colonial practice of displaying Native American culture as fixed objects of the past, therefore contributing to the ongoing erasure of native people by implying that they no longer exist.

Along with the central presence of sexual, gender and ethnic minorities in the avant-garde of performance art, the 1980s were also an important decade for formal experimentation. New York-based Taiwanese artist Tehching Hsieh (b. 1950) made his five one-year performances between 1978 and 1986. These were one-year-long pieces in which the artist blurred the boundaries between performance art and everyday life. In the first, Hsieh lived in a cage for one entire year without speaking, reading, writing or watching television, and with nothing more than a single bed, a wash basin and a pail. In later pieces, he punched a time clock every single hour for a year, lived completely outdoors in Manhattan with a backpack and a sleeping bag for a year, and spent one year tied to performance artist Linda Montano (b. 1942) with an eight-foot-long rope. In the last of these pieces, Hsieh spent a year without creating or consuming any art. Hsieh's one-year pieces, which explored questions of solitary confinement, discipline, endurance and privacy also constitute examples of *durational performance*. These are works that unfold over a sustained period of time and in which the time of the performance and the time of everyday life overlap.

A contemporary of Hsieh, William Pope.L (b. 1955) has also thoroughly explored the possibilities of durational performance. Beginning in the 1970s, he has engaged in over forty endurance-based 'crawls' during which he dragged his body onto streets, sidewalks or gutters. In one of the most notorious of these pieces, 'The Great White Way', Pope.L crawled the twenty-two-mile-long Broadway in New York City in different segments over the course of five years wearing a Superman costume and a skateboard strapped to his back. Playing with absurd or ridiculous images and using the urban space in creative ways, Pope.L's performances called attention to the experience of being a black man in white capitalist America.

EXTREME BODY PERFORMANCE

Throughout the history of performance art, many artists have experimented with pushing the physical limits of the body through self-inflicted pain, self-mutilation, body modifications and the exposure of bodily fluids that society deems unsuitable for public view, such as blood, excrement or semen. By foregrounding the body's vulnerability to harm, these artists may seek to reach different mental states and provoke visceral reactions in the audience. Works that fall under the label of extreme body performance are often rebuked by critics and audiences as having no artistic value other than shock, or are directly attacked for their supposed ability to morally corrupt audiences. And yet many of these works are worth considering precisely because in making us uncomfortable, they might offer deeper insights into the interplay of sexuality, identity, embodied experience, objectification and violence.

Artists have been experimenting with extreme body performance since the beginning of performance art. In his 1971 work 'Shoot', Chris Burden (1946–2015) stood against a wall in front of a small audience as a friend standing about fifteen feet away shot him in the left arm with a rifle, after which he was taken to a hospital. In Burden's words, his performance aimed to show that 'being shot is as American as apple pie', and that guns are an important part of American culture. Because of these statements, some critics and audiences have arguably overestimated Burden's intention in this piece to make a political commentary about the ubiquity of weapons in American society. In fact, 'Shoot' was only one piece in a broader body of work in which Burden's main goal was to explore different forms of physical danger and pain. Even though his work, especially 'Shoot', remains a notorious early example of extreme body performance, some critics have argued that Burden's work ultimately served to reify for audiences his agency over his pain and the inviolability of his white, male, abled body.

Although Burden's 'Shoot' remains an iconic piece in histories of extreme body performance, later artists have pushed the boundaries of the genre. Extreme body performance by female, queer, disabled and/or people of colour artists complicates notions such as agency, identity, body integrity and physical suffering because their bodies are always already perceived as objects of desire and violence. A seminal figure in extreme body performance, Ron Athey (b. 1961) started his career in the 1980s with experimental pieces he performed in the queer underground club scene of Los Angeles. He gained popularity in the 1990s, performing work that drew aesthetically on sadomasochism and Christian iconography and explored themes related to masculinity, homosexual desire, trauma and HIV activism. Athey's work was heavily informed by his HIV-positive status, his upbringing in a family of fundamentalist members of the Pentecostal church as a gay child, and his youth years of depression and drug use. Athey's work has since gained international recognition, and yet it has tended to remain marginal in accounts of American performance art. His status as an uncomfortable artist for many critics and audiences made him one of the central figures around which the controversies of the so-called 'culture wars' developed in the 1990s.

In 1994, Athey performed 'Four Scenes in a Harsh Life', commissioned by the Walker Art Centre in Minneapolis. This piece was part of his *Torture Trilogy*, which also included 'Martyrs and Saints' (1992) and 'Deliverance' (1995). In one of the scenes, Athey carved signs on the back of fellow performer Divinity Fudge (Darryl Carlton) with a scalpel and used paper towels to soak up the blood. These 'prints' were then hanged on a system of strings that hovered above the audience. Scandal emerged after a reporter who had actually never been at the show wrote about the performance in a sensationalist tone, suggesting, for instance, that HIV-infected blood dripped on the audience. Despite the fact that Carlton was HIV-negative and no dripping took place, the story circulated in the media and was later picked by Christian conservative organizations and right-wing legislators. Overnight, Athey became a figure that crystallized the worst anxieties of conservatives about obscene art, moral decadence and the dangers of extending rights to sexual minorities. Republican senator Jesse Helms took the story to Congress, using Athey as a scapegoat to justify defunding the National Endowment for the Arts and fuelling homophobic moral panic for political gain. The controversy made it hard for Athey to present work in the United States for years and prompted his move to Europe, where he consolidated his status as a leading figure in contemporary performance art. Despite public opprobrium and constant accusations of obscenity – and also because of them – Athey's performance work captures many social processes that were taking place in American society during the AIDS crisis, from homophobia and the stigmatization of HIV-positive people to the pain of those who had to see their loved ones die as public policies to support HIV research were insufficient.

Like Athey, other artists have prolifically used blood in their performance work. London-based Italian performer Franko B (b. 1960) predominantly used bloodletting in the majority of his work from the 1990s and early 2000s. In these pieces, Franko B bled from wounds or catheters inserted into his body, often covering himself in white body paint that drew all the more attention to the bright red blood. In his 2003 piece 'I Miss You!', performed at London's Tate Modern, he walked naked and covered in white paint on a white canvas that resembled a runway while blood dripped from his arms and onto the canvas. Stopping at the end of the catwalk each time to be captured by the cameras of the attending photographers, Franko B let blood accumulate at its feet. He repeated the walk back and forth until visibly weakened and straining from the blood he was losing, provoking visceral reactions in the audience. Franko's performance evoked the physical agony one experiences after love is lost, but also brought up questions about compassion and anxiety, as well as the ethical responsibility to intervene that spectators might feel towards a person who is bleeding out in front of their eyes.

Queer theorist and art critic Jennifer Doyle has made the argument that Franko B's 'I Miss You!' and its display of sentimentality constitutes an intervention in the politics of institutional art spaces where too much emotion is discouraged. She argues that, traditionally, these art spaces favour a supposedly higher critical approach from which one is encouraged to absorb art only conceptually, always keeping a distance and without getting carried away by emotions. In opposition to this, artists such as Franko B and Ron Athey are eminent examples of what Doyle has named 'difficult art', which is art that engages spectators through emotions that might be hard to experience and invites them to interrogate the political reasons for their reactions.

Even though extreme body performances by artists such as Ron Athey and Franko B explicitly exhibit the suffering body in ways that both echo and interrogate notions of masochism, not all extreme body performance necessarily foregrounds physical suffering. For instance, Cyprus-born Australian performance artist Stelarc (b. 1946) turns to robotic anatomical structures, medical technology and virtual reality to expand the human physical limits and enhance the body's capabilities. In his performance work, he has used a robotic third arm, been connected to electrodes that remotely stimulated movement in his muscles, used a six-legged spider-like robotic machine as an exoskeleton, and had a human ear cultivated from cells surgically implanted in his arm. By using technology that can radically alter the human body, his work highlights the vulnerability of the body in the face of systems that outperform it, and consequently, points to both the anxieties and the promises inherent in developing these technological systems.

Among the canon of extreme body performance art, French artist ORLAN constitutes a somehow exceptional position due to the fact that her work has tended to celebrate the possibilities of contemporary medicine to transform the body. Between 1990 and 1993, ORLAN had nine face-altering plastic surgeries, grouped together under the name of 'The Reincarnation of Saint ORLAN'. Some of these surgeries were recorded and televised for audiences. The artist was given different forms of local anaesthesia that allowed her to remain fully conscious and watch what the medical team was doing with the help of mirrors. ORLAN's work differs from other extreme body performance artists in that rather than working with the experience of pain, she fully embraces the possibilities offered by medicine to avoid it altogether.

Despite what conservative and fear-mongering detractors of extreme body performance might argue, its purpose is not to shock audiences or corrupt society. In fact, the works grouped under this label raise important questions that are explored in performance practice and scholarship and that are not so much meant to be answered as reflected upon. Among other questions, from a performance studies perspective we might ask: What are the differences between extreme body performance art and other extreme physical practices, such as religious self-flagellation and self-harm inflicted as a result of trauma? Are these phenomena clearly separated from each other or do they overlap in significant ways? What might their commonalities tell us about the nature of pain, bodily integrity, self-determination and the ethical implications of witnessing someone's pain? What are the limits of empathy for performance audiences? How do we make sense of spectatorial discomfort, and what are the causes of our discomfort in the first place? After all, disgust, abjection, pain, etc., are an integral part of our lived experiences, and though difficult or unpleasant, these feelings have a valid place in artistic experimentation. Moreover, difficult feelings experienced by the audience of a performance piece often point to aspects of the human experience that cultures repress under veneers of propriety. Part of the work of performance studies scholarship and practice is to explore difficult spectatorial experiences in order to open up discussions about which identities and bodies are deemed abject, disgusting, obscene, undesirable, dangerous, or vectors of contamination, and why.

PERFORMANCE ART AND CAPITALISM

Artists engaging in body art in the 1960s and 1970s understood their work as a break with many of the conventions of the art world, including its most commercial tendencies to treat art like any other commodity that could be bought and sold on the capitalist market. For these pioneers of performance art, refusing to let their work be commodified was also an ideological stance, as they opposed what they perceived to be the most complacent dimensions of bourgeois art spaces, where audiences engaged in superficial consumption of art instead of being transformed by it. Instead of catering to this bourgeois complacency, they thought, body art could serve to awaken the critical consciousness of the public and address injustices. And indeed, many of the formal qualities of performance art that we have discussed throughout this chapter seemed, at the time, able to save it from commodification. The focus on the creative process rather than the final art object, providing audiences with unique experiences, performing outside of institutional art spaces such as galleries, museums or big commercial theatres were all characteristics that made each performance art piece a unique event that was hard to monetize. From a contemporary perspective and just a few decades later, these early hopes seem almost naïve, and performance art seems perfectly suited to satisfy the art market's demands for innovation and works that are perceived to be innovative, fashionable or edgy.

Changes in the structures of art funding since the 1980s in many Western countries that had prominent performance art scenes, such as the United States or the United Kingdom, are also part of this shift. As a result of increasingly relying on private and corporate models of arts patronage and slowly dismantling previous models that subsidized art as a domain of public interest, the arts currently function more like a business and, in turn, performance artists and their work function more like commodities. Like all contemporary art-makers, performance artists need to take into account the taste of corporate funders and institutional grant-givers who often value artists and works that can draw in money as part of cities' tourist attractions and urban development plans for art districts. As wealth disparities grow in society at large, they are also growing in the performance art world, creating a landscape in which consolidated institutions and specific names can make a lot of money while artists and organizations at the lower end of the art market can barely generate enough money to survive.

Unlike a few decades ago, when performance art was an incipient genre, contemporary capitalism has found plenty of ways of packaging and selling unique and unrepeatable experiences as commodities. Marina Abramović's (b. 1946) piece 'The Artist is Present', is a paradigmatic example of an artist whose performance work has achieved the status of highly sought commodity on the art market. Performed in 2010 at the Museum of Contemporary Art in New York City as part of her retrospective, the piece was a durational performance in which Abramović sat at a table during the hours the museum was open for the three months of the exhibition. Spectators waited in line to sit in front of her for a few minutes, often experiencing a heightened state of emotion. The performance was greatly mythicized by media coverage, particularly a viral video circulating on social media that depicted Abramović's encounter with her former life and art partner Ulay (1943–2020), who teared up looking into her eyes. While Abramović's purpose was to create a personal, emotionally intimate encounter with each spectator, arguably the piece's meaning and popularity was derived from her status as an international performance art star. The status of this performance as a commodity also became apparent in the speed with which it became something of â cliché, even generating subsequent well-circulated parodies, the most popular of which was a video that circulated on Facebook and which depicted Ulay crying in front of a pug puppy standing in for Abramović.

Richard Schechner's recent critique of the performance avant-garde in his book *Performed Imaginaries* is pertinent to discussing the contemporary commercial dimension of performance art. Schechner points out that the repetition of performance pieces that were edgy a few decades ago has been a recent phenomenon in the art world. But whereas in their first appearance these pieces were pushing against the boundaries of what was considered acceptable art by audiences and art institutions, their most recent revivals function as mainstream products that, far from unsettling any boundaries, are revered as classic pieces in the performance art canon. Schechner sees a certain nostalgia taking place in these revivals, specifically in the way these pieces might be perceived as relics from a past in which performance art was deemed capable of enacting social change, as opposed to a contemporary view of performance art as much less ambitious in its political agenda. His argument is that even though the artists participating in these revivals might personally hold progressive politics, the art they make does not seem to advance the agenda of progressive politics at all. To be sure, Schechner does not personally blame these artists as much as the nature of the art industry in contemporary capitalism. One might be tempted to dismiss his critique as the perception of an established figure who seems to think the past was more radical and edgy than the present. However, the celebrity achieved by performers like Abramović and the media attention they draw suggest that Schechner is onto something. This does not mean that performance art is incapable of pushing boundaries in our contemporary moment, but that artistic practices that emerge in the margins of institutions often have to let go of a lot of their radical goals and agendas in the process of becoming celebrated in the mainstream art world.

Part of the job of performance studies is to not assume that performance art is inherently radical because it is formally risqué or because of the stated intentions of its creators. Rather, performance studies is interested in the effects that particular examples of performance art might have at particular times for particular audiences. We might ask: What social processes are we able to better understand by looking at the ways bodies in performance create meanings? Why is it important to reflect on the discourses surrounding performance art when it is done by sexual, gender, racial or disabled minorities? And what boundaries might performance art be breaking when creating not only communion, joy or celebratory participation in its audiences, but also confusion, resistance, discomfort or disgust?

FURTHER READING/RESEARCH

Johnson, Dominic. *Pleading in the Blood: The Art and Performances of Ron Athey.* Intellect Live. Bristol: Intellect, 2013.

Piper, Adrian. *Out of Order, Out of Sight*. Cambridge: MIT Press, 1996.

Roth, Moira, and Mary Jane Jacob. *The Amazing Decade: Women and Performance Art in America, 1970–1980*. Los Angeles: Astro Artz, 1983.

Vergine, Lea. *Body Art and Performance: The Body as Language*. Milan: Skira, 2000.

Warr, Tracey, and Amelia Jones. *The Artist's Body*. London: Phaidon, 2000.

If interested in exploring performance art practice, choose one of the 'event scores' in Yoko Ono's book *Grapefruit* and follow the instructions.

3

PERFORMANCE AND PERFORMATIVITY

REPETITION AND RE-ENACTMENT

The activities we can describe as performance do not only refer to the staged artistic events that we find in art galleries, museums, theatres, concert halls or under the umbrella of performance art. In the domains of business, science and technology, performance describes the carrying of an activity according to certain standards, such as when we talk about the performance of stocks over a period of time, or the performance of an electric car battery. In sports, performance is often used to describe qualities of both spectacle and function, for example, when a football player performs a successful play on the field. In common parlance, performance can be used both pejoratively to signify that someone is putting on an act, showing off, or being disingenuous, and positively to commend someone's prowess at a given task. In a more general sense, performance is a constitutive element of human behaviour, as the process through which human cultures are formed and identities forged. Performance is often called a 'contested concept' because of the plurality of meanings it can take and the different social and cultural practices it describes.

A helpful way to think about all of the things we have described as performance is that they entail some form of embodied repetition. Therefore, to perform an action is to repeat or recreate that action. This is obvious in the way actors rehearse for their performances in film, television or on stage, often repeating gestures and text intonations over and over until getting the perfect form. But it is also how everyday performance works. Every performance, from a quotidian crossing of legs while sitting on a bar stool to the triple axel jump of

DOI: 10.4324/9780429286377-4

an Olympic figure skater, is in fact a re-performance, a repetition of some previous performance. This is why performance studies scholar Richard Schechner has defined performance as 'twice-behaved' or 'restored' behaviour in his book *Between Theatre and Anthropology*. By this, he means that human behaviour is formed by recombining fragments of behaviours borrowed from someone else, who in turn recombined fragments of behaviours from a third person in an endless chain of performances that travel between bodies. Performance simply cannot exist without repetition. Michael Jackson's signature moonwalking is not the exact same movement when any other person tries it, or for that matter, was not even the exact same movement every time he performed it, and yet all instances of moonwalking ever performed are recognizable as the same movement pattern, the same behaviour repeated and – one might say – restored by thousands of bodies. If I were to stand from my desk and attempt to moonwalk as I am writing these lines, I would be engaging in an actual repetition of moonwalking, a rehearsal of sorts, even if I had never personally done it before. This is because the behaviour has existed and circulated by and between bodies for a long time before my actual enactment of it.

The paradox of the mechanism of repetition inherent in all performances is that it both perpetuates and changes them. A hundred different actors can play Hamlet using the same stage blocking, costume, gestures and text intonations, and while all of them would create the same Hamlet performance, they would also, in fact, create a hundred different Hamlet performances. Some of them would likely be better than others based on subtle changes that each actor would introduce as they repeat the same behaviours. In fact, if we were to watch them all, some would surely seem better than others even if it were hard to pinpoint exactly why. This is because embodied performances are never repeated in exactly the same way. As it travels from body to body, repeated behaviour is, in some sense, both different and new each time, both repeated and transformed, both the same and different, both old and new.

This tension between repetition and difference is at the core of performance. In fact, the success of different kinds of performances often depends on where they fall in that imaginary spectrum between repetition and difference. For a queer teenager trying to pass unnoticed in a religious conservative community, minimizing the difference between their gender performance and the expected social norm might be precisely what makes their performance succeed. The more exactly they repeat the behaviours that are considered 'masculine' by family and neighbours, the more likely they are to blend in. For a campy drag queen, the simultaneous performance of femininity and its carefully staged 'failure' – its difference from an actually convincing performance of femininity – can be the source of an audience's elation. In one case, the difference has to be minimized; in the other, it is exaggerated. In both cases, gender performances are enacted through repetition of certain behaviours, though with very different stakes. Both performances happen on almost opposite positions of the spectrum between exact repetition and noticeable difference. Literary scholar Linda Hutcheon has argued that 'repetition with a critical difference' is the base of parody. To understand what she means, one only need to think of any successful comedian impersonating a celebrity, politician or historic figure. The success of such performances lies in a skilful balance between repeating the original behaviour with enough similarity as to make it recognizable, while introducing enough distortion as to make it comedic.

A lot of canonical theories in the field of performance studies have grappled in some sense with this tension between repetition and difference that operates in performance. The theory of twice-behaved behaviour posited by Schechner is one example. Other theories, some of which we will review in this chapter and the next, have talked about performance in terms of re-enactment or reproduction. Re-enactment, as in the acting out of past events at historical sites or museums, is at its base the repetition of extraordinary events or everyday behaviours from a historical past. Repetition and difference are also at the base of definitions of performativity. As discussed in this book's first chapter, repetition and difference constitute the base for Jacques Derrida's and, later, Judith Butler's theories. Derrida believes it is repetition that gives the force to performative behaviour. Butler emphasizes repetition in her theory of gender performativity as the social mechanism that conditions one's performance of gender. After all, we are able to understand a particular behaviour as feminine or masculine when we see it performed precisely because we have seen different versions of it before, on other bodies, on screen, on stage, or in real life, perhaps much earlier than we can consciously remember.

The very repetition of our identity performances is also what makes them real and natural to us.

While for some performance studies scholars, repetition is what defines performance, for others, performance is precisely that which cannot be repeated. For those in the latter camp, performance is the ephemeral and unique live event that happens in real time and then is forever lost. The following section examines the debate between these two positions.

LIVENESS AND MEDIATION

For some people, especially in a world so thoroughly mediated by technology as ours, live performance has the appeal of being an 'authentic' experience. We often hear people say that you 'had to be there' to understand the 'magic' of a live concert, the 'impact' of a performance art piece, or the 'charisma' of an actor on a theatre stage. Some performance studies scholars have actually argued that this liveness, this quality of being unrepeatable of an event happening in the here and now, is precisely what defines performance. Chief among the scholars taking this approach is Peggy Phelan, who in her book *Unmarked: The Politics of Performance* has argued that performance can only exist in the present because when it is recorded and circulated through media it becomes something altogether different. Adopting Phelan's perspective, it follows that mediated performances, that is, instances of performance that circulate through technologies of reproduction such as television, internet, phones, etc., are just copies of real live events. For Phelan, the inability to be reproduced is the strength of live performance, because it avoids being packaged and endlessly distributed as a commodity under capitalism. Live performance, therefore, offers a kind of resistance to commodification. One might agree with Phelan in principle and recall instances of live performance that felt like unique and wonderful experiences precisely because of being aware of their ephemerality. However, one might also question the idea that live and mediated performances stand in opposition, that mediated performances are derivative while live performances are originals, and that performance only lives in the present. Isn't going to a concert, recording it with a phone, and posting live fragments on social media a once-in-a-lifetime kind of experience, made possible *precisely* by technological mediation, and not despite of it?

Some performance studies scholars have extensively argued against Phelan's view that performance only lives in the present. Philip Auslander, in his book *Liveness: Performance in a Mediatized Culture*, takes issue with those who see live performance as a site of cultural resistance in a mediatized society. Instead of seeing liveness and mediation as an either/or issue, Auslander argues that the boundaries between live and mediated performance are blurry, because many live events are created with the intention of being reproduced or directly incorporating technologies of reproduction, such as big concerts that could simply not happen without sound technology and massive screens that amplify the performers' image. Auslander also thinks that the mediation of performance makes it potentially accessible to many people, while traditional live performance venues, such as theatres, art galleries and concert halls, uphold cultural privilege by only reaching a small population of elite consumers and connoisseurs. Moreover, Auslander believes that the appeal of live performance is possible precisely because of the invention of technologies that could reproduce it, particularly film. It was only when performance could be endlessly reproduced and circulated that people started appreciating the live event and reflecting on its special characteristics. Or, in other words, without mediation it would make no sense to speak of 'live' performance; it would be just 'performance'.

Even though Auslander is right in that, in contemporary society, live and mediated performances are often not clearly separated, the question of whether live performance provides a unique set of experiences for spectators is still worth considering. A main shortcoming in Auslander's argument is that it presupposes a spectator that engages performance only visually and aurally. He is not wrong, because sight and hearing are the predominant – and often only – senses that staged performances in the Western tradition solicit from its audiences. However, there are forms of performance for which other sensorial dimensions, such as touch, taste and smell, are a crucial part of the participants' experience. These other sensorial dimensions have not yet been successfully mediatized through technology. An immersive sensorial experience that engages all senses is still unique to live performance and accessible only through the embodied presence of performers and audiences in the here and now. This is true even when these performances might also include all sorts of technological mediations through microphones, sound systems, cameras, screens, etc. Both critics and audience members attending some extreme body performance works by Franko B and Ron Athey, for example, have described the olfactory dimensions of blood and sweat as being essential to their experience of the event. And arguably, we can extend this uniqueness of experience to performance art pieces that do not readily appeal to smell. Every performance piece for which the audience's participation is imperative, or for which the interaction with audiences *is* the performance, such as Ono's 'Cut Piece' and Fusco and Gomez-Peña's 'Couple in the Cage', both mentioned in the previous chapter, provide unique live experiences regardless of their afterlife when recorded and circulated through media. And yet, Auslander is absolutely right that the quality of being live is neither necessary for performance to be considered as such, nor should it be considered the root of a performance's appeal. General arguments about the 'magic' experience of all live performance and its ability to create a 'community' of spectators are more often than not just romantic appeals to physical presence in a society dominated by media. To be sure, performance is capable of creating unique experiences, but this ability of performance is hardly conditional on it being live.

Another argument to counter Auslander's critique of liveness is that his analysis applies exclusively to performance understood as staged aesthetic practices. But what about other forms of performance that do not take place on stage? As I am writing this book, after an entire year of the COVID-19 pandemic and the experience of successive lockdowns, it is hard not to argue that there seems to be something unique to the human psyche that makes us feel connected and grounded when we communicate through live embodied encounters – or at least when a good part of our social performances take place live. Everyday social performances like a birthday toast with friends, a romantic date, a wedding celebration or a family holiday meal seem to demand liveness. These events require our physical embodied presence in space and time because they demand more from our bodies than just watching and hearing. This seems to suggest that, while highly applicable to staged performances, Auslander's argument that liveness is not a necessary condition of performance is less applicable to rituals, celebrations or performances of everyday life.

Feminist performance scholar Rebecca Schneider offers yet a different viewpoint, arguing that both Phelan and Auslander are limited in their view that live performance only happens as an immediate experience, and never as a recording device in its own right. In *Performance Remains*, Schneider invites us to consider a different perspective: What if the body in live performance is also a recording technology, a form of archiving the past? Basing her discussion on historical re-enactments of the US Civil War, Schneider demonstrates that reenactors precisely perform and re-perform their battles as a form of keeping the past alive. Their live performances are not just immediate unrepeatable experiences that take place in the present and then disappear, nor do they need technology in order to be archived and reproduced. Rather, in historical re-enactments, live performance *is* the means of recording the past. The ongoing repetition of the live event becomes the archiving technology that is able to conserve the historical event and make it endlessly accessible.

Yet another viewpoint in this debate comes from José Esteban Muñoz, who talks about the 'burden of liveness' that those belonging to minority groups have historically endured. Muñoz refers to the fact that, while access to public life and political representation has been often denied to people in these groups, they could participate in public life as spectacle. Performing on stage for the aesthetic consumption of the white heteronormative majority was often the only way in which individuals from racial, ethnic or gender minorities were allowed to have a public presence at all. When considered from this perspective, liveness in performance is not a magical quality but a burden.

Even though it might be tempting to equate performance which that which happens live, the theories discussed in this section productively complicate that equation. When all these theories are put in dialog, we realize that liveness might be necessary for some social performances, that some live performances might provide unique experiences to their participants, and that nothing suggests that liveness is a necessary condition of all performances. In other words, as Auslander points out, an event does not need to be live in order to be a performance and, as Schneider suggests, the liveness in live performance does not even have to be circumscribed to a one-time event, but might rather be an ongoing repetition. Such questions about liveness and mediatization have been and, to a certain extent, still are fundamental to the field of performance studies. For someone encountering these debates for the first time, they might even seem overrepresented. Yet there is a reason for this: once the study of performance turned from studying dramatic literature or texts to studying bodies and events, questions about performance liveness, mediatization, ephemerality, disappearance, remains, presence, permanence, recording, archives and archiving practices became central to the field. This is because, while dramatic texts could be approached as more or less static objects of study and were assumed to remain constant even when scholars' interpretations of them changed or evolved, bodies and events are never static.

SPECTATORSHIP, COMMUNITY, PARTICIPATION

For the greater part of Western history, the audience of staged performances had a more or less defined role as external observers who watch what happens on stage from a rather passive position. Even notably vocal or disruptive audiences, such as Roman crowds clamouring for the pardon or execution of a gladiator in the circus, or Elizabethan spectators throwing rotten fruit at the actors on stage, were still largely limited to watching what was offered to them and reacting to it. Starting in the twentieth century, many avant-garde artists and performers explicitly experimented with forms of disrupting the passivity of audiences and breaking the *fourth wall* – the imaginary separation between performers and spectators. German director and playwright Bertolt Brecht (1898–1956) wanted to promote the audience's critical engagement with the social situations of injustice presented on stage. French dramatist Antonin Artaud (1896–1948) sought to engage spectators in visceral and emotional experiences that would shake bourgeois notions of propriety and decorum. Brazilian theatre director and political activist Augusto Boal (1931–2009) used theatre for civic engagement inviting spectators to go onstage and dramatize everyday life conflicts affecting their communities. However experimental, these and other examples were still circumscribed to an understanding of performance as staged practice, even as they were often blurring boundaries between theatre, music, dance, poetry and visual art. As performance studies became a defined field of inquiry and the meaning of performance was broadened from staged practices to a much larger set of social and cultural phenomena, the notion of audience or spectatorship also had to be re-examined and redefined.

By taking a broad approach to performance, performance studies complicates traditional definitions of audience, spectatorship, participation and community, and understands that partaking in performance can happen in a wide variety of forms. The believers who gather in the Vatican square to attend mass by the Pope, the customer who pays for a lap dance in a strip club, the feminist protesters demanding the legalization of abortion in Argentina, or a historical re-enactment in colonial Williamsburg that invites participants to behave as if they were living in the eighteenth century, to name just a few examples, cannot simply be contained by the same terms of engagement and definitions of audience. From a performance studies perspective, many situations that can be described *as* performances tend to blur the boundaries of categories such as spectator, audience, community, activists, participants and performers.

Performance studies rarely considers audiences to be just passive observers. The very relationship between audiences and performers in real time is what creates much of performance art. Performance theorist Erica Fisher-Lichte has defined this phenomenon as the 'autopoietic feedback loop', which means that performance art happens in real time as a process of interaction between performers and participants. To put it differently, a theatre company can perform *Macbeth* whether there are a hundred people in the audience or none. Surely the energy in the theatre will be very different and we can speculate about what is even the point of performing without any spectators, but we can agree that *Macbeth* as a play can happen without audiences and has an existence beyond the gathering of particular audiences. But without people willing to sit in front of her and hold her gaze, how would 'The Artist is Present' be any different from Marina Abramović just spending time sitting at MoMA on any given day?

Performance artists may plan some of the conditions or circumstances of audience engagement, and really talented ones provide a structure under which a successful – interesting, meaningful, unusual, perplexing, etc. – encounter happens with spectators. For example, in his 2007 performance 'Domestic Tensions', Iraqi-American artist Wafaa Bilal locked himself for a month in a prison cell-like space in a Chicago art gallery, offering viewers the option of watching him twenty-four hours a day through a webcam, communicating with him through a chat room, or remotely activating a paintball gun to shoot at him at any time. By setting the terms of how audiences could interact with him in these ways, Bilal ended up revealing the ease with which some viewers took the opportunity to exert violence on his body. Arguably, the point of the performance was precisely to show how easily latent violence would become explicit and enacted on the body of an Iraqi man in United States in 2007, and without the spectators' willingness to shoot at him, there would be no such performance. Like Bilal, many performance artists invite their audience into a relationship in their own terms, or like Tehching Hsieh during the last of his one-year performances mentioned in the previous chapter, they might refuse the terms of the relationship altogether, but once they enter this temporary relationship, they cannot control all its outcomes. In this sense, performance art as an event is unrepeatable because it is open to the real-life interaction and, like Phelan would argue, if it were to be recorded or happen again it would be absolutely different. From this perspective, terms like 'audience' or 'spectators' do not even begin to describe the relationship between participants in the performance event. Many performance artists invite participants into roles that go well beyond hearing or seeing, the two terms that are etymologically linked to audience and spectatorship.

The question of the audience gets even more complicated as we abandon a limited definition of performance as artistic practice and include any instance of performance as repeated or 'twice-behaved behaviour'. For if there is nobody there to see a particular behaviour, is it a performance or is it simply 'being'? Are we performing any social roles when we are alone? And who is the audience for our gender performances when we are not in front of people? One might argue that there is no performance outside of the realm of communication, and that realm involves at least two parties. This is largely true, except that for most people their gender expression does not change whether they are in front of others or by themselves.

Even if nobody is watching, the audience has been internalized by the subject who performs. We can think of this audience as society at large and the expectations about proper behaviour that come with living in it. In other words, for our identity to be performative, one of the two parties involved in the process of communication might not even need to be present at all for performance to occur. In this case too, it seems that what we are talking about much exceeds terms like audience or spectatorship.

Many performance studies scholars have also been interested in the potential of live performance to provide for participants a collective experience of community. This idea originates in the work of anthropologist Victor Turner's definition of *communitas*. As mentioned in this books' first chapter, this is a collective experience during ritual ceremonies or rites of passage in which participants feel like a community of equals, even if their everyday social positions are in fact distributed in a clear social hierarchy. Because of this momentary experience of community, participants can see glimpses of other possible social arrangements, presumably more egalitarian ones, that lie beyond the existing social structure. After Turner, other scholars have explored how performance might provide experiences of community. In *Utopia in Performance: Finding Hope at the Theatre*, feminist scholar Jill Dolan talks about 'utopian performatives', which are small but powerful moments experienced in live performance that emotionally engage audiences and stimulate their imagination and their desires for a better future. In Austinian fashion, Dolan believes that the 'performative' in utopian performatives makes the vision of a better world present and palpable for spectators. She astutely points out that the experience of spectatorship might extend beyond the theatre and animate larger political projects or civic participation. While Dolan refers mainly to live performance happening in theatrical settings, other scholars have extended this analysis to other kinds of performance, such as the dance club. Performance studies scholar and one of Dolan's former students, Ramón Rivera-Servera, in his book *Performing Queer Latinidad: Dance, Sexuality, Politics*, argues that performance activates political change in queer Latino dance spaces. Though often ephemeral, the experiences of community generated in the dance club can provide participants with a critical and emotional experience that they might use to different political ends. For Rivera-Servera, communities that emerge in performance are not so much based on clear identity boundaries but on desires, common political interests and shared experiences of oppression. These communities are not given categories but alliances formed through performance.

We will talk more about the relationships between identity, performance and community as it pertains to sexual, gender, racial and ethnic minorities in the following chapter. For now, it is enough to repeat the idea that scholarly perspectives in performance studies such as the ones provided in this section render the idea of spectators and audiences as passive observers of performance completely obsolete.

PERFORMANCE, PERFORMATIVITY AND THE PERFORMATIVE

As stated earlier in this book, linguistic theorists such as J. L. Austin and John R. Searle brought attention to the ability of performative speech to shape the world, Jacques Derrida emphasized the weight that social convention has in this process, and Judith Butler shifted the focus of performativity to identity, particularly gender. Drawing on these foundations, performativity has been further taken up by thinkers concerned with understanding how identities are formed in processes of negotiation between inherited social conventions and individual acts, between automatic repetition of taken-for-granted behaviours and actions that disrupt them to bring about change. This section delves deeper into performativity and how it is understood in performance studies, before we move to a more thorough exploration between performativity as it pertains to identity in the next chapter.

Interestingly, when positing his theory of performative speech acts, Austin completely excluded theatre and language that happens on stage. He believed that, since performance in the theatrical sense only 'pretended' to be reality, dramatic language could never constitute performative speech acts. This is why actors playing characters who marry onstage are not married in real life, and people sentenced to death in a play do not actually have to die. Reproducing the old Platonic anti-theatrical prejudice that saw staged performance as a mere copy of real life, Austin did not think that performance could have any performative value. In fact, he went as far as to describe theatrical language as an 'etiolation' of language, that is, a decadent, lacking and abnormal version of language. Despite Austin's insistence in separating performativity from performance, the relationship and the differences between the two terms have been thoroughly explored in performance studies and in the academy at large, prompting some scholars to say that a 'performative turn' happened in the humanities in the 1990s.

At the forefront of this performative turn, we find gender and queer studies, two fields that are deeply related to performance studies. Austin's disregard for language uttered on stage as etiolation is discussed by Andrew Parker and Eve Kosofsky Sedgwick in the introduction to their 1995 edited volume *Performativity and Performance*. Both scholars of literature, gender and queer studies, Parker and Sedgwick argued that Austin's particular choice of the word 'etiolation' tied performativity with queerness since the very beginning, ascribing theatricality to a category of the peculiar, exceptional, non-serious and even abnormal. Along with many other queer theorists, Sedgwick and Parker turned to performativity for its ability to explain the social dimensions that influence identity, particularly queer and non-normative identities, in relationship with heteronormative social expectations. Before her premature death to cancer in 2009, Sedgwick became a seminal figure in establishing queer theory and queer studies in the American academy. She was particularly interested in studying how certain linguistic structures might reproduce or unsettle heteronormativity. Exploring speech figures such as silence, secrecy and disavowal and the ways they relate to experiences of shame and paranoia, Sedgwick attempted to shed light on how queer individuals experience and react to heterosexuality. In addition to writing extensively about queer performativity, Sedgwick also mentored students who would become leading figures of queer theory and performance studies such as José Esteban Muñoz.

The 'performative turn' popularized among linguists, philosophers and literary theorists who were concerned with gender and sexuality, such as Butler, Parker and Sedgwick, was received by other scholars of performance with a certain scepticism. They worried that turning attention to performativity, a linguistic theory, was the latest of a centuries-old academic tendency to cast the study of embodied practices as secondary to the study of texts. Performativity, for them, offered plenty of opportunities for abstract theorizations of identity that were ultimately disembodied and unconcerned with actual performance and lived experience. Theatre and feminist scholar Elin Diamond argued that conversations about performativity must be grounded in particular instances of performance or they would become too abstract. And performance ethnographer Dwight Conquergood, whose work is explored more extensively in the last two chapters of this book, famously wondered what would 'get lost' in the study of performance by equating performativity with the citation of social norms in line with Derrida and Butler. He worried that, in explaining identity formation in the abstract, performativity would overlook embodied particular lived experience while also deemphasizing the role of performance as a force of social transformation. If performativity was understood primarily as the process through which peoples' bodies recite or enact social norms, what about the ways in which bodies perform to contest and disrupt social norms? Following postcolonial theorists, Conquergood empathized a view of the *performative* as that which contests and opposes hegemonic cultural forces. The performative element of culture, for him, was composed of those forces that resisted and reversed social hierarchies and various forms of oppression.

Whether one understands performance as artistic practice, staged event, cultural tradition, everyday social behaviour or embodied expressions of identity, performativity is a useful theoretical tool in understanding how social norms are both materialized and contested on the body through repetition. These social norms shape peoples' embodied behaviours and might in turn be resisted through embodied behaviours. Norms include actual laws enforced through legal coercion, vernacular customs, cultural habits, moral values, religious beliefs, etc. During the pre-Civil Rights era in the United States, for example, racial segregation in public spaces was a rule enforced by law and racist violence, and also made real through everyday performative behaviours as white and black people sat in different parts of the bus, used different restrooms, attended different schools and shopped at different businesses. When Civil Rights activists such as Rosa Parks refused to give up their seat in the 'white' section of the bus, or insisted on sitting at 'whites-only' business counters, they were enacting a different performative and disrupting the social norm.

Performative disruptions, however, do not always take the epic, highly visible route of the Civil Rights movement. And performative norms that shape our bodies and identities are not always as readily identifiable as the regime of racial segregation enforced by Jim Crow laws in Southern United States. Often, the performative dimension of everyday behaviours that derive from and consolidate power structures is much more subtle. For example, before 'manspreading' became a popular hashtag on social media under which women posted pictures of men sitting with legs wide open on trains and flights, this generalized gendered behaviour was mostly unnoticed. There are uncountable everyday examples we can think of in which someone's presence in certain public spaces might make other people more comfortable or uncomfortable, and that respond to habitual unexamined behaviours. How might, for instance, quotidian walking patterns through busy city streets reinforce social hierarchies that make a homeless person invisible as hundreds of pedestrians pass by without giving them as much as a glance? In our daily activities, we all enact and negotiate our positions and differences in power relations depending on our identities. We do so through performative behaviours that come into play in a web of social conventions that we often ascribe to without giving it a second thought. Performative behaviours, however, are not set in stone. Just as they become normalized by repetition, they can also be disrupted and performed differently.

Now that we have delved a little deeper into definitions of performativity, a couple of questions might come to mind: How does performance relate to performativity? And where do the two terms intersect and differ? Using the most elemental definitions we could say that performance is a framed event or action with communicative purpose while performativity is the embodied citation of behaviour resulting from processes of socialization and that is naturalized by repetition. But the two terms inform each other in several ways, at least from a performance studies perspective. First, performativity always manifests through performance, as habitual and socially sanctioned repetitions of behaviour crystallize in individual action, gesture, movement, intonation, etc. For example, gender is performative but its performativity can only be appreciated as such when gender behaviour becomes actualized in individual performance. This means that we understand that gender is performative as a theory *because* we are able to look at the world and see real people embodying behaviours that to us look gendered, whether feminine, masculine, gender-fluid, non-binary, etc. By the same logic, we can appreciate how specific gender performances might comply with or rub against social norms in a given setting. We could argue that there is no performativity without performance, as there is no gender without the embodied acts that make it present and material on people's bodies. This is what feminist critic Elin Diamond meant when she argued that performativity is always materialized in performance and that, without attention to performance, performativity risks becoming an abstract theory without much grounding in people's lived experience.

Second, even though in order to analyse performance it is useful to think about it as a framed event with discrete time and space limits, the truth is that every performance conjures up a broader universe of previous performances and future potential ones. In other words, performance events are themselves performative in that they are individual acts in chains of behavioural repetition. This is true of theatrical performance, which in its relationship with reality presents things that are recognizable as representations of the world. It is also true of cultural and social performances, such as rituals, which are performative because they derive their efficacy and social recognition from having been repeated for a long time. Various forms of protest and political struggles also constitute good examples of this relationship between the unique performance act and its belonging into a performative tradition. A Black Lives Matter demonstration in 2020 echoes and reinscribes not only similar demonstrations from recent years, but also past race struggles from the Los Angeles riots of 1992 to the Civil Rights movement of the 1960s, and black liberation struggles worldwide. Adopting a performance studies perspective to look at such events allows us to see them as different actualizations of historical forces that have been going on for a long time. From this perspective, every protest or demonstration cites and repeats elements of previous ones, draws inspiration from the past, refines and reshapes its strategies to adapt to the present, and opens up possibilities for future movements. One could define this as a performativity of protest performances that is tied to a group's subordinate or minoritarian position within a social domain, something that is covered more in depth in the chapter dedicated to performance and activism. This is yet another way to think of performativity as citation or repetition, one akin to what Dwight Conquergood underlined in his discussion of the performative.

Third, even when adopting a narrow definition of performance as a bounded event that showcases an aesthetic or artistic practice, performance can be a powerful means of reflecting on, negotiating and contesting the underpinnings of performativity. This means that in performance we are often offered the chance to critically examine the weight of social norms. As explained in the previous chapter, this is one of the main lessons offered by the history of performance art as an artistic genre. As feminist and queer performers of colour from the 1970s onward used their performance practice to bring their gender, race and sexual identities to the fore of public culture, they opened up conversations about how bodies are viewed, how they signify, and how they disrupt social conventions. Performance, in these cases, provided occasion to peek into the mechanisms of performativity and to point to its ability to consolidate social hierarchies.

PERFORMANCE FAILURE

As mentioned throughout this book, in addition to asking what performance *is*, the field of performance studies is concerned with what performance *does*, that is, what is accomplished in various social and cultural domains through performance. Taking at face value the assertion that performance does things in the world, almost immediately raises the spectre of its opposite: What does performance not do, or rather, what does performance fail to do? In which circumstances does performance fail? And more broadly, what does it mean for a performance to fail? As we close the chapter, this section offers speculative answers to these questions.

There are a few different ways in which we can talk about performance failing. In the simplest of senses, a performance arguably fails when it displeases its audiences or participants. This can happen when audiences recognize a performance as such but do not like its execution, such as when one witnesses a performance of *Hamlet* and dislikes the acting. In this case, the performance has failed to do what it presumably set out to achieve, that is, deliver a satisfactory version of the Shakespearean classic by a specific set of standards of artistic achievement. Performance might also fail when one who purportedly came to see a performance sees something that they cannot accept as having any value as a cultural product. This would be the case of a conservative spectator appalled by an example of extreme body performance who refuses to call what they just saw 'art'. In both of these cases, all parties involved agree that what is happening is a performance, but disagree about its worth. But can we confidently say that the performance in the second case has failed? What if the scandalized spectator's reaction was part of the artists' goal to provoke negative feelings in the audience? What if the risk of alienating some part of the audience seemed to the performance artist a necessary price to pay for the content they wanted to create or the issues they wanted to explore?

Another criterion for defining performance failure might refer to performances that fail to appear as a performance altogether. This is arguably a failure of the performance's framing. To continue with examples from the genre of performance art, we could say that spectators who saw 'Couple in a Cage' and believed to be in the presence of *real* caged indigenous people failed to recognize that they were witnessing a performance. However, if this very act of misinterpretation makes the performance relevant by proving that colonialism continues to structure our perceptions of cultural difference, can we consider that the performance failed? In other words, wasn't this failure to recognize the performance as such precisely part of what the performers were counting on to prove their point? Did the performance fail for just the group of spectators who didn't see it as such? If so, was it necessary for the performance to fail in this way for some spectators so that it could succeed for the rest?

Beyond the realm of staged or artistic performance, defining performance failure becomes an even more arduous task. In the work of J. L. Austin, an 'unhappy performative' is that which fails to do what it set out to do because at least one of the things that were supposed to happen for the performative to be successful went wrong. Taking again his classic example of the marriage ceremony, among the things Austin lists for the procedure to go wrong are incorrect or incomplete execution, execution by the wrong or unauthorized people, or procedures abused by participants who utter the right words but do so without sincerity. If any of these things happen, the procedure is botched and the performative has failed.

After Austin, other theorists of performativity have talked about failure in a more capacious way, allowing room for the productive possibilities that might arise from a failed performance. For Judith Butler, the failure to conform to the norms of socially accepted gender behaviour is precisely what reveals the existence of the norm. In other words, because some people are signalled out for not performing gender in normative ways, we can begin to understand the social norms that enforce normativity. And understanding these norms is no small step in the process of dismantling some of their most oppressive consequences. José Esteban Muñoz has explicitly valourized performance failure and the possibilities it can generate. Muñoz talked about a 'queer aesthetic of failure' that often appears in the performances of punk musicians or drag performers. This failure should not be equated with a lack of success but with a personal aesthetic choice that these performers set out to explore as part of their practice. What is 'queer' about this kind of failure, for Muñoz, is its refusal of the 'normal' and its desire to escape from it, where 'normal' stands in as capitalist exploitation and conformity to heteronormativity. Muñoz wisely prompts us to ask: Can performance fail and still produce something good in that very failure? For Muñoz, performance is an instrument that minoritarian subjects – people whose identities mark them as minorities in society – use as a strategy to distance themselves from dominant values and imagine better futures. The ways in which performance might be strategically used by minoritarian subjects to resist hostile dominant culture is one of the main topics explored in the next chapter.

FURTHER READING

Hamera, Judith. *Opening Acts: Performance In/as Communication and Cultural Studies.* Thousand Oaks: Sage Publications, 2006.

Jones, Amelia, and Adrian Heathfield. *Perform, Repeat, Record: Live Art in History.* Bristol; Chicago: Intellect, 2012.

Parker, Andrew, and Eve Kosofsky Sedgwick. *Performativity and Performance.* New York: Routledge, 1995.

Rivera-Servera, Ramón. *Performing Queer Latinidad: Dance, Sexuality, Politics.* Ann Arbor: University of Michigan Press, 2012.

4

IDENTITY AND LIVED EXPERIENCE

PERFORMANCE, REPRESENTATION AND VISIBILITY

Aside from repetition and re-enactment, two topics covered in the previous chapter, it can be helpful to also think of performance as *representation*. This is especially true if we adopt a narrow definition of performance as artistic practices that happen onstage, in films, and in other media, as well as performance art and forms of performance that are clearly framed as artistic works even when they happen in spaces outside of traditional theatre and art circuits. In its most basic sense, a representation is the depiction or portrayal of something or someone. However, representation is never just a mere copy of the world or a transparent window into it. Representations offer depictions of the world from particular viewpoints. This is true of representations that depict completely fictional worlds, such as the Wakanda of the Marvel Cinematic Universe that is home to the superhero Black Panther, as well as representations of actual or historical events, such as the assassination of black revolutionary socialist Fred Hampton – a real life Black Panther – by the FBI in 1969, as depicted in the 2021 film *Judas and the Black Messiah*. Documentaries and news reporting created with outmost informative rigor and striving to provide neutral facts also constitute particular representations of the world. Even representations that seem completely far-fetched are somehow related to reality. Representations both stem from and circle back on the real, seeming believable to us because they conjure up in some form what we already know to be true and offering ways to make sense of the world around us.

DOI: 10.4324/9780429286377-5

More than any previous time in human history, contemporary global society relies heavily on the circulation of representations through visual culture and multiple media. The importance of visual culture in shaping human perception is a phenomenon that first became prominent in the twentieth century with the ubiquity of film, television and video images. In the twenty-first century, as even the most basic of our daily tasks are mediated through screens, our immersion in visual culture and its ubiquitous representations of the world has been exacerbated. Because of their prominent presence in our lives, representations shape how we see the world.

Adopting performance as an object of analysis and performance studies as a methodology helps us understand how representations function, how they circulate in society, and how they affect people. The effects of representations are particularly relevant when they relate to power dynamics and hierarchies existing in society, a prime concern for the field of performance studies. Performance studies cares about representation in the sense that Jamaican-born British cultural theorist Stuart Hall (1932–2014) pointed out when he said that the way people are represented is the way they are treated in society. In lay terms, this means that performance studies pays attention to how certain groups, identity traits and power relations are portrayed in literature, film, theatre, art, advertising, the news and even scientific, medical, juridical and philosophical texts, and believes that these representations have a performative power in society and that they affect how people are thought of and treated. Negative, oversimplified or partial representations of certain groups and identity traits are neither innocent nor do they exist in a vacuum. For example, depictions of Native Americans in classic Hollywood westerns as belligerent, savage, connected to nature and animals and prone to scalp their enemies are directly related to how the United States as a country understands the history of its expansion west in the nineteenth century as a process of civilization against wilderness. And one does not even have to go as far as classic Hollywood westerns to realize that portrayals of Native Americans as full-fledged human beings are exceptional even in contemporary media. Examples of partial or questionable representations of minorities abound, constituting a powerful example of how representations influence everyday life. One of the crucial aspects of representations, as we will see throughout this chapter, is how they depict difference, and therefore how they effectively influence our understandings of racial, ethnic, sexual, gender, class and ability differences.

Because how people are represented is inextricably connected to how they are treated, one might be tempted to believe that an abundance of positive representations about a particular group or identity trait would suffice to improve the forms of oppression that afflict these groups. In fact, a common trope in modern politics and public discourse is that social progress comes from having more people from marginalized or minority groups in positions of power. This is supposed to both inspire other people in marginalized positions to aspire to success and convince those who stand in the way of these groups' success of their humanity. In this view, increasing the *visibility* of marginalized groups in public life has unquestionably good consequences. The problem with this theory is that it grossly oversimplifies and misunderstands how representation relates to power differences existing in society. Critical scholarship on the intersections of race, gender, class, sexuality and ability has made it clear that offering positive representations of oppressed groups without changing the conditions of their oppression can only go so far. For example, a multinational retail corporation that profits from the exploitation of poor women of colour who make their clothes in developing countries for meagre wages cannot really contribute to the emancipation of women of colour, even if women of colour in the West were to constitute the majority of its executive board and stakeholders. In a similar vein, a country that fails to implement policies that guarantee access to affordable housing, education, healthcare and living wages to black people cannot magically change those conditions by electing a black president.

More importantly, directly equating more visibility or more positive representations of individuals from marginalized groups with better social conditions for those groups is a mistake because visibility is never neutral. In fact, visibility and representation can be quite effective instruments of oppression. People from oppressed groups have never been invisible to begin with, but are very likely to stand out in public spaces that do not welcome them. The cases of black people being questioned, harassed and often brutalized by police forces for just being in majority-white neighbourhoods are but one example of how certain groups can be both highly visible and yet simultaneously disempowered by that very visibility. Perhaps more importantly, visibility and representations are influenced by dominant forms of visuality. *Visuality* is the way in which what we see with our eyes is interpreted and given meaning. Like language, visuality is socially constructed and functions according to a set of rules that one is acculturated into since birth. Visuality both depends on existing social structures and helps maintain them. Specific examples of this were provided when discussing the history of feminist performance art in a previous chapter. Pioneer women performance artists who were deploying their bodies in explicit ways were never completely outside of the male gaze that dominates society and practices of art spectatorship. Within those given conditions, however, they were attempting to reclaim their bodies from an artistic tradition that had portrayed the naked female body as a passive object of male contemplation and to present themselves also as authors and creative and political personas. Beyond performance art, this struggle with the terms of visibility affects minoritarian identities across the board, as people belonging to marginalized groups have historically used a plethora of performance strategies to reclaim visuality, a subject we will explore more thoroughly in following sections. Performance, therefore, can and has historically served to both reify and subvert negative representations, often being a negotiation between the two.

When we talk about performance in relationship with the representation of difference, we need to also take into account how performance has been pejoratively ascribed to certain bodies. White women and people of colour have always been suspected of performing excessively. In the comparison of femininity and masculinity, whereas the latter is seen as neutral, the former is seen as the gender of performance, artifice, spectacle and make-believe. From make-up and hairdos to cat-walking and sultry voices, being feminine is supposed to involve props, costumes and rehearsal. Because the feminine gender is considered inherently performative, there is always the suspicion that women can be duplicitous and manipulative. In fact, the trope of a woman who uses her beauty to charm and subdue a male hero is surprisingly consistent throughout diverse cultures, from ancient tales to modern melodramas. Masculinity, in contrast, is still widely regarded by many in society as neutral, natural and devoid of artifice. This unexamined tendency to see femininity as a performance in patriarchal societies acts in subtle but ongoing ways even in progressive spaces. This may explain, for instance, why drag queen performers and their performances are much more predominant and visible in mainstream culture than drag kings, who remain a marginal genre in the drag world and mostly unheard of in mainstream culture. With the increased popularity and success in popular culture of drag performers such as RuPaul and the many notorious drag queen contestants from his homonymous Drag Race, it seems that millions of spectators around the world find a biological male putting together a show of femininity a very compelling thing to watch, while its opposite not so much.

Performance has also been pejoratively ascribed to black and indigenous people as well as all people of colour. Racist and colonial histories that equated people of colour with nature and irrationality saw their existence as exclusively embodied – meaning it was never their 'being in their body' that was questioned but rather their having a mind at all. Dance, music, embodied rituals, heightened forms of expressivity and, in general, performance, was supposed to naturally belong to non-white people. Black people have been especially affected by these racist notions. As a legacy of the slave trade, in the trans-Atlantic world black people occupied roles of entertainers and live performers and put on the spotlight as a spectacle to be consumed even when performance was one of the only means of participation in public life that they were afforded. Recall that in the previous chapter this was discussed as the 'burden of liveness' experienced by people of colour, in the words of José Esteban Muñoz. The history of blackness as a spectacle to be consumed means that black performance in the public sphere has always existed in dialogue and tension with racist legacies. Blackness itself is often regarded as spectacular and worthy of consuming as a source of entertainment. Despite the now-dominant social consensus that it is deeply racist, blackface minstrelsy casts a long shadow. One only has to see the controversies that in the last years some notorious young white male YouTubers have faced for their blackface performances, which they justified as just innocent and humorous impersonations of the stereotype of the sassy, loud, over-the-top working-class black woman. Blackness, in this justification, is conceptualized almost like a funny costume that one can put on in performance for assured laughs.

The fact that blackness is always already seen as a performance implicitly renders white bodies, by comparison, as non-performing, and therefore less histrionic or dramatic. This is why scholar of African American literature and performance Saidiya Harman has coined the term 'hypervisibility' to describe the experience of being black in relation to visibility and representation in society. One could certainly argue that the trappings of being both looked at and invisible also affect disabled bodies, an argument made by scholars of performance and disability studies such as Petra Kuppers. The same could be said of bodies who do not conform to cisgender norms. The transphobic obsession with describing trans people as cross-dressing or performing an identity that is not their biological one further proves how entrenched these prejudices are. In this sense, we could say that the most 'invisible' performances in both the art world and society at large are those delivered by white men when they perform as themselves. Talking about white male identity performances in terms of invisibility does not refer to their lack of success, but quite the opposite. By passing as non-performance, performances of white masculinity manage to secure their ubiquity in every position of power, in every realm of society while remaining largely unnoticed. By remaining under the radar as non-theatrical and non-performative, white masculinity represents the neutral norm against which all other performances of identity are measured and deemed noticeable. This is why, for people belonging to a minority group, gaining visibility in society does not always necessarily mean gaining more power.

To explain the illusion of why whiteness and masculinity are widely regarded as neutral and natural identities, performance studies scholar Peggy Phelan has developed the concept of the 'unmarked'. Like other feminist critics concerned with the relationship between representation, visibility, and power, Phelan argues that, just like language exists prior to one's learning of it, so does the visual field – the ways in which one looks and is looked at. And just like language, the visual field is also organized by particular rules. A main rule is that representation is almost always on the side of the person who looks, and not on the person who is seen. This rule applies to representation in the visual field in art, painting, photographs, film, etc., which have historically been organized as if the person looking were by default a white heterosexual man. Because of this socially constructed dimension of the visual field, gaining visibility for those who are underrepresented can be a futile attempt to distribute power, especially if this increased visibility does not entail a profound examination of who is required to display what and for the enjoyment of whom.

Phelan illuminates that the viewer is the position that remains unmarked and this position can hold a lot of power. A classic example of this is found in the work of feminist film critics of the 1970s such as Laura Mulvey and Teresa de Laurentis. These feminist film critics realized that images of women in film were not constructed to represent the woman as a subject, but to represent her as an object within a visual field of male desire. The camera positions and movements depicted the woman's body as if a heterosexual male were looking at it. This was so even when no man was in the scene with her, implicitly putting the spectator in the position of the man who looks. In turn, for male spectators this consolidates their gaze on the woman as object. For female spectators, what gets potentially consolidated is the habit of seeing women, including herself, through a male gaze. Though later queer theorists also questioned these early feminist film theories for only including heterosexual desire in their study of how films structure the gaze, the point remains that visual culture can reinforce a dominant power position through apparently inconspicuous representations.

In opposition to the power that comes with looking, Phelan also enumerates some of the potential traps that come with increased visibility for groups who have been historically under-represented. These traps include surveillance, fetishism, voyeurism and sometimes death. In other words, if the structures that determine the power differences in society do not change, giving more visibility to under-represented groups might be also increasing the ways they are exposed and vulnerable in relationship to those in power. Phelan points out that the contemporary insistence on visibility politics, that is, on increasing representations of the under-represented, is perfectly compatible with capitalism's appetite for new markets. Following Phelan, one can think about the ways in which brands use celebrities of colour to target customers within the same demographics. More visibility for the under-represented often implies more opportunities for corporations to sell them things. For example, one can speculate that, from the perspective of the film industry, the worldwide distribution of the *Black Panther* movie is as much related with capitalizing on the millions of black people willing to pay for the movie ticket and the merchandise as with racially diversifying existing representations of superheroes. In this sense, providing representations of the pan-Africanist utopian society of Wakanda and depicting black models of empowerment is a means through which the Marvel Cinematic Universe extends its market to black consumers. This can be true at the same time as spectatorial experiences of the film can feel empowering for black people. The truth is that we do not have to choose between these two positions as if they were mutually exclusive. In contemporary capitalism, they coexist. This section has explored how performance as representation can both reify and contest dominant forms of seeing difference. The following section delves more deeply into how this is related to identity.

PERFORMANCE AND SUBJECTIVITY

While it is true that positive representations and increased visibility do not suffice to overhaul the conditions that oppress people belonging to minorities, they are still important in an individual's development. Representations shape a person's subjectivity, that is, the way in which they make sense of themselves, their identity and their relationship with the world that surrounds them. Never seeing people with which one can identify is a problem, and so is seeing people with which one can identify being mostly represented in demeaning, oversimplified or abject ways. The importance of representations in the shaping of one's subjectivity is a process that starts early in childhood and continues throughout an individual's entire life. Many scholars interested in the relationship amongst visibility, representation and subjectivity base their work in essential findings in the field of psychoanalysis. Although psychoanalysis is a vast and complex field with numerous contributions, for the purpose of this section it is sufficient to say that early psychoanalysts like Sigmund Freud (1856–1939) and Jacques Lacan (1901–1981) were concerned with understanding how and when human babies develop the knowledge that they are an autonomous subject different from their caretakers. Lacan's 'mirror stage theory', for example, posits that when the human baby sees their own reflection in a mirror, they start developing the awareness of how they look from the outside, therefore how they look to other people. After Lacan, later experiments found that while other animals, such as baby chimpanzees, also seem to understand that the reflection in the mirror is them, humans are unique in that they are the only species truly fascinated by their reflection. Leave a human baby in front of a mirror and they will spend a lot of time moving, gesturing and reacting to what they see. Psychoanalytic theory believes that this behaviour is at the base of how humans come to understand themselves through an external gaze, that is, how a human individual comes to understand how other people see them. For a species as social as ours, taking one's behavioural cues from others has been an essential means of survival.

Later research in human development has found that the human infant develops feelings of shame for behaviour that fails to elicit a response in their caretaker, and tends to repeat behaviour that does. The caretaker's response becomes essential for the infant to develop their sense of self, and important aspects of their personality such as self-worth, confidence, assertiveness or trust in others. There is strong evidence to suggest that, for the human infant, forming a subjectivity is a process of both understanding themselves as a different entity from others and finding others they can identify with in the world around them, both processes that start in early age through interactions with caregivers and keep developing in adult life. If we extrapolate these findings from the contained scenes of babies in front of mirrors and caregivers' reactions to infants to human behaviour as a whole, we might begin to understand why how one is being looked at and what one sees in others is so important for human subjectivity. At the base of these finding in psychoanalysis and human development we find what feminist performance scholar Elin Diamond has called 'looking-at-being-looked-at-ness', or the ability of humans to understand themselves simultaneously through both inner and outer cues. A human individual knows themselves as a coherent self in a double process, looking to the outside and looking at themselves as if from an outside perspective.

Representations of identity and difference circulating in society are therefore deeply entrenched in how people learn to look at each other and themselves. Starting in early childhood, representations of difference such as gender, race and sexual identities, for example, shape the ways in which we understand and expresses ourselves as gendered, raced and sexual beings. The individual is not a contained unity, but a porous being that forms alongside, within and against the images of self that one can identify with in the outer world. Individuals develop their inner sense of self through constant exchanges between their looking at the world and being looked at, between their own expressions and the available representations they can identify with or against in the environment, between behaviours seen and behaviours enacted. But what does this mean for those who have historically occupied oppressed positions in society, those for and of whom representations have been inexistent, partial or outwardly demeaning? Are these individuals invariably trapped by negative representations in the way they make sense of themselves? Do they have any agency in changing or counteracting these negative representations?

Performance scholars and practitioners have thoroughly explored these questions. As explained in the previous section, representations are not neutral but are deeply embedded in a visual order that is socially constructed. However, representation also conveys more than it seems. This is especially true of representations in performance, art, film, etc., that is, of representations that convey aesthetic dimensions. This happens because when we have an aesthetic experience, we do not only access it through rational thought. Our whole body, our senses, our memories, our emotions, our desires, our special awareness are engaged in the experience. This is why representations, even when deeply entrenched in dominant visuality, can often hold space for alternative interpretations beyond those conditioned by socially established modes of seeing. Performance studies scholars such as Daphne Brooks, Nicole R. Fleetwood or José Esteban Muñoz have explored what happens when minorities of colour are authors and recipients of their own representations. In *Bodies in Dissent: Spectacular Performance of Race and Freedom*, Brooks looks at popular entertainment genres from the mid-nineteenth century to the first decades of the twentieth century, such as magic shows, theatre, cakewalk dancing or equestrian shows, among others. Brooks demonstrates how African American entertainers used these staged performances to present their bodies in public in ways that resisted conventional views of blackness existing in society at that time.

Fleetwood extends this perspective to contemporary culture. In *Troubling Vision: Performance, Visuality, and Blackness*, she argues that blackness is always represented as a problem in visual culture and examines contemporary black cultural producers who have attempted to trouble this perspective. Of particular interest is her discussion of black female cultural producers who strategically deploy performances of 'excess flesh' to comment on mainstream representations of black women. Fleetwood notices that, as a legacy of slavery, in the transatlantic imagination, black women's bodies have always been depicted as excessive. Excessive in their sexuality, their expressivity, and the space they take, black female bodies served as a prop to define everything that was ideal and desirable in white women by contrast. Whereas ideal white women were depicted as respectable, proper, poised, chaste and compliant, black women were depicted as precisely the opposite. Fleetwood argues that black women cultural producers that deploy 'excess flesh' do not necessarily perform liberation from these cultural stereotypes, but rather call attention to this deeply entrenched and problematic imaginary construction of the black female. Fleetwood analyses both elite cultural forms, such as visual art, performance art and photography, and pop culture figures such as Janet Jackson and Lil' Kim. We could certainly extend Fleetwood's definition of 'excess flesh' to other contemporary black women performers beyond her case studies, such as Nikki Minaj, Cardi B and Megan Thee Stallion. In their intentional use of hypersexualized images of black women, we find plenty of room for pleasure, agency and a sense of empowerment beyond negative representations of oversexualized black femininity. Performances of excess flesh such as these are not always unproblematic or liberatory, but they do make room for other possibilities in representations of excessive black female bodies.

Both Fleetwood and Brooks talk about black performance as enacting a sort of 'alienation' from socially constructed representations of blackness. This means that these performers playfully engage existing representations of blackness and disavow them at the same time, suggesting to the spectators that they can both inhabit the stereotype and be at a distance from it, that the stereotype does not define them. These forms of alienation also resonate with what José Esteban Muñoz has called 'disidentifications', a process through which minoritarian subjects form their identity in dialogue with dominant cultural representations. Instead of complete identification with available representations or counter-identification that outright opposes these dominant representations, disidentification in a third option. It is simultaneously an aesthetic strategy that Muñoz finds present in the work of queer artists of colour such as film maker Isaac Julien, painter Jean-Michel Basquiat, conceptual artist

Félix González-Torres, performance artists Carmelita Tropicana and Marga Gomez and drag performer Vaginal Davis, among others, and a form of reception of their work for queer of colour audiences. For the artists, disidentification often uses toxic and phobic representations of minoritarian subjects and re-works them through satire, parody and humour, as well as gaudy, campy and over-the-top aesthetics. Muñoz offers examples such as black drag queen performer Vaginal Davis' 'terrorist drag', in which they perform in white face as a homophobic militiaman from Idaho, or Carmelita Tropicana's playful self-identification with *chusma*, a derogatory term that in Cuban vernacular is often used against poor people of colour to convey improper, excessive and hypersexual behaviour. In adopting these tropes, these performers disidentify with them, working within these representations and manipulating them to suggest other meanings.

For Muñoz, disidentification is a survival strategy that works simultaneously within and outside the dominant public sphere. This survival strategy might not always be ideal or work for everybody, but it allows minoritarian subjects to avoid having to choose between compliance with and outright confrontation with a hostile public sphere. Through disidentification, queer of colour subjects neither assimilate within the dominant social values nor strictly oppose them, but rather transform the dominant cultural logic from within. Muñoz argues that disidentificatory performances work against the tenets of heteronormativity, white supremacy, and misogyny that are dominant in mainstream society. Against these values, disidentificatory performances strive to activate new social relations and imagine possible futures for queer of colour liberation. A lot of the performances Muñoz posits as examples of disidentification are from the 1990s, when the AIDS pandemic had been ravaging queer of colour communities for two decades and right-wing sectors of society were waging culture wars and attempting to enact discriminatory legislation against these groups. In this historical context, disidentification was a strategy to use the aesthetic realm to imagine possibilities for queer of colour survival and thriving against very demoralizing historical circumstances.

Performance scholars such as Brooks, Fleetwood and Muñoz acknowledge the problems that representation and socially dominant forms of visuality pose in the formation of subjectivity for people belonging to minorities. These scholars, however, are also invested in finding the ways in which minoritarian subjects can use performance to resist these representations, or at least engage with them in ways that do more than just reify the dominant power relationship implicit in representation. They think of performance as an experimental, productive instrument that allows the minority subject to negotiate, express, experience and embody possibilities that are outside of the available dominant scripts for representation. By and large, this is a view of performance that has been dominant in the field of performance studies. More recently, other performance studies scholars have started questioning the limits of performance as a productive instrument in representation. Among these contributions, Kelly Chung invites more caution with the idea that minoritarian identities are knowable in representation and performance. Looking at art and performance both produced by and representing women of colour at work, Chung argues that performance cannot always offer transparent access and understanding into the experiences and subjectivities of these women. When representations of women of colour at work remain abstract, partial and indeterminate, they fail to satisfy our spectatorial hope that performance will offer us access to an other's experience of oppression. Instead, what we experience is performance's very inability to offer this access.

While in this section we have discussed performance and its relationship with representation, in the following section we will delve into the relationship between performance and lived experience.

PERFORMANCE AND LIVED EXPERIENCE

What is expressed in performance is deeply related to human lived experience. Because of our social nature, human beings feel the need to express many of our experiences as a part of processing and sharing them with others, a process that often happens through performance. From everyday conversations, gossip and jokes, to more elaborate expressive and artistic forms such as song, dance, music, film, theatre or performance art, performance is the expression of human experience. Performance and lived experience are connected in a feedback loop, such that what we experience as individuals is given form and social existence when it crystallizes in performance. In turn, performances that are socially shared by a culture create the sedimented habits and behaviours that make human identity. This feedback loop between performance and lived experience is what creates cultural specificity. Performances are culturally specific when they arise from the lived experiences, histories and traditions of a particular group of people. The musical genre of blues, for example, cannot be divorced from the lived experience of African Americans in the south of the United States in the second half of the nineteenth century. Blues incorporates African musical forms, alongside black spirituals, slave work songs, field hollers and an entire sonic universe of shouts, notes, rhythms and vocal textures. It constitutes a unique, culturally specific form of expression because it emerges from the lived experience of the people who created it. Culturally specific performances also take on a life of their own when they travel beyond the local domains in which they are created. To continue with the same example, blues circulates in the world through performance, occupying public space, becoming commercialized in particular music works and artists, reaching different times and locations, finding diverse audiences and evolving. In this circulation, performance can also be copied, appropriated and deployed in contexts very different from the ones in which it was created. It can also adapt and transform into other musical genres, like blues transformed into rhythm and blues and rock and roll. In its circulation, culturally specific performance can be appropriated as an expressive form by mainstream society, a topic we will explore more in depth in the next section as we rehearse debates about cultural authenticity and cultural appropriation. However, even as it crosses time, spaces and audiences, performance has the ability to carry the specifics of the lived experience from which it emerged. This relationship between performance and lived experience as described in blues is not unique. It applies to all culturally specific forms of expression that particular human groups create and share.

While paying attention to the ways in which performance circulates and evolves, performance studies has also tried to understand what is characteristic of performance as it relates to the lived experience of people whose identities have been forged in resistance to systems of oppression. The role of performance as result and bearer of lived experience occupies a particularly important place for groups whose existence has been historically threatened, endangered or severely limited by extreme acts of violence, such as genocide. In *Spectacular Suffering: Theatre, Fascism, and the Holocaust*, Vivian Patraka has talked about a 'Holocaust performative' that, faced with the impossibility of representing the Holocaust as a fixed and complete narrative, survivors engage with through performance. In Patraka's examples, theatrical performance becomes a way of making meaning of the incommensurate pain and loss of genocide, an attempt to deal with the psychological breach produced in trauma through theatrical representation. Judith Hamera has also discussed the relationship between trauma and performance for survivors of the Khmer Rouge genocide in Cambodia, one of the case studies that comprise her book *Dancing Communities: Performance, Difference, and Connection in the Global City*. In Hamera's ethnographic research with a family of Khmer refugees relocated to Long Beach, California, Cambodian classical dance is the primary means of negotiating trauma. But the relationship between trauma and performance that she offers is not one of healing and overcoming. Rather, re-performing the movements of their classical dance technique was for these subjects experienced as both a duty to preserve a culture lost to genocide and a source of frustration for the impossibility to fix idealized past cultural forms through embodied performance. What is true in both Patraka's and Hamera's accounts is that performance becomes an embodied attempt by survivors to make meaning of traumatic events that overwhelm the usual human psychological mechanisms of meaning-making.

For indigenous and native populations around the world, as well as the black populations connected through a history of slavery and African diaspora, performance and expressive culture has often been a source of knowledge and cultural resistance to capitalism, colonialism and white supremacy. Black performance studies, for example, examines what is characteristic to black aesthetic and black sensibility, and how performance constitutes blackness as an identity through performative forms such as black speech, black musical improvisation, black visual art and black literature. Black performance, however, is not merely defined by histories of oppression, but also by the worldmaking capacities that have allowed black people to imagine better futures in performance. Performance studies scholar E. Patrick Johnson refers to black performance as a form of knowledge, meaning that black performance has provided black people with the means to know themselves and their culture, and to reflect on the different dimensions of the black experience. The black church service and black musical traditions are two prime examples of this. But if performance is a site for the expression and often celebration of blackness and resistance amongst black people, the entirety of the black experience and black identity also exceeds its performance. This means that the experience of being black is also more than what can be expressed in performance. According to Johnson, blackness is also a material mode of knowing and living in the world that supersedes performance and the spectacular representations of black identity that are found in performance. Blackness, in this sense, is also lived experience that cannot be captured in performance and that resides in the black psyche and the black way of experiencing the world.

This notion of lived experience that might exceed its ability to be translated into performance points to the limits of understanding identity through performative models. This means that not every aspect of identity might be as easily explained by adopting a performative model as gender is. Race is performative, but upon closer examination of discussions of race in both society and sociological discourse, it becomes apparent that race is not performative in the same ways gender is. While transgender experiences have become more visible in society at large, the very notion of a transracial experience, that of individuals who assert a racial identity different to that of their birth, makes many people rightfully uncomfortable. Indigeneity as an identity category also seems to fit uneasily into performativity. Kānaka Maoli (Native Hawaiian) scholar Stephanie Nohelani Teves has noted the resistance of people within native and indigenous communities to notions of their identity being performative. Colonization and ongoing exploitation of indigenous land and resources in settler colonial societies such as the United States, Australia and New Zealand already constructs native and indigenous identity as hybrid, mixed and waning out. In this view, current indigenous populations are already deemed less 'authentic' versions of their indigenous ancestors, which in turn seeks to delegitimate their claims to land. Many native and indigenous people fighting against this ongoing colonial construct of their identity find the notion of a performative identity to further expose their culture to disappearance and erasure. Teves argues that performance studies as a field still has a lot to learn by listening to the ways in which native and indigenous populations represent themselves and their identities. The fact that some identity categories such as race and indigeneity don't quite fit seamlessly into performative understandings of identity poses interesting problems for the field of performance studies. The next section delves into some of these problems, as we discuss performance in relationship to debates about cultural authenticity and cultural appropriation.

PERFORMANCE, AUTHENTICITY AND CULTURAL APPROPRIATION

As discussed throughout this chapter, from a performance studies perspective, identity is not so much a series of essential traits that an individual is born with but a series of behaviours that the individual performs in relationship with socially constructed categories. This means that identity categories such as masculinity, femininity, blackness, whiteness, queerness, indigeneity or whatever other categories we can think of do not just have fixed universal and biological meanings. Rather these categories are socially constructed through cultural scripts and representations, and the expressive acts performed by individuals. They can change over time and present local particularities in different cultural contexts. These cultural scripts create power differences between groups of people based on embodied characteristics. These cultural scripts are also historical, meaning that they derive from past relationships between groups of people and keep evolving. For example, one is not essentially 'white' and 'male', as if the meaning of white male existed in nature, or as if people had understood those categories in the same way across geographical location since time immemorial. Rather, one performs whiteness and maleness in relationship to dominant cultural understandings of gender and race that have been historically created to disenfranchise people belonging to other categories such as 'black' and 'female'. This means that biological differences such as sex and phenotype, which exist in nature simply as the variety of characteristics that the homo sapiens presents, have been historically arranged in social hierarchies and ascribed different value through cultural processes. Therefore, performances of race and gender are determined by socially dominant understandings of race and gender.

The fact that identities are socially constructed categories, does not mean that an individual person can pick and choose their identity or how to perform it, or that they can fully change the social script through their individual performance. One cannot choose to be or not to be black, white, gay, straight, disabled, etc. Culturally created differences between groups of people have a life of their own, seeming natural and fixed. Though socially created, individual performances of identity are internalized as natural and perpetuated by individuals through repetition. At the same time, the individual is not completely powerless in their performances of identity, as these performances of identity can both reify and contest the dominant cultural scripts and representations, as we have seen throughout this chapter. In the end, identity is a series of performative acts through which the individual negotiates between the available cultural scripts and their own process of performing those scripts.

Because identity is performative, one cannot be authentically white, authentically black, authentically female, authentically trans, authentically Asian and so on, for what does 'authentically' even mean in each of those cases? Nevertheless, discourses about such authenticity abound in society. Individual performances of identity are evaluated in relationship to abstract ideals and arbitrary standards of identity. Former United States president Barack Obama was often accused of not speaking like a black person. But how does a black person speak? And was Obama any less black because he did not perform the black vernacular speech that is commonly associated with African Americans? In contrast, if he did not speak as a black person, what race did he speak as? Speaking of white authenticity, for example, always unveils histories of racism, genocide and white supremacist political projects. Though less obviously problematic, investments in black authenticity are often deployed in black communities also with exclusionary purposes. Scholars of black performance, such as E. Patrick Johnson, have made the argument that normative blackness in the United States has been historically used to exclude gender non-conforming black people and sexual minorities from black communities. Exile, immigrant and diasporic youth born or raised to foreign parents in Western countries often face accusations of being less authentically part of the original culture that their parents. Because of the way they speak, dress or have diverged from the home country customs, they are accused, even by their own communities, of being less authentically Mexican, less authentically Jamaican, less authentically Algerian, less authentically Korean and so on. But appeals to authenticity do not only happen in service of questionable or racist projects. Strategic appeals to essentialism and authenticity can serve as a rallying cry for a community to come together. For working class people of colour in a rapidly a gentrifying neighbourhood, appealing to authenticity can be a form of organizing against gentrification, the white-washing of their neighbourhood and urban displacement.

The paradox of cultural authenticity is that debates and considerations about authenticity become all the more predominant precisely because identity is performative rather than fixed. However, as soon as one probes the criteria through which performances of cultural authenticity are evaluated, authenticity starts falling apart. The fact that the criteria through which authenticity is established is often arbitrary, however, does not preclude people from feeling very strongly about the topic. Authenticity in relationship to identity stirs powerful emotions and strong opinions. One's performance of identity is perceived as more or less authentic and this can have serious consequences. From politics to popular culture, notions of authenticity have often served to exclude more than include people. In any case, authenticity is a social discourse about a person's performance of identity, often deployed to evaluate that performance for different projects. The politics of claiming authenticity or accusing someone of not being authentically something are complicated.

Claims about authenticity in performance often bring up the issue of cultural appropriation. The careers of prominent white rappers such as Eminem, Macklemore and Post Malone have developed amidst accusations of appropriating black culture. Prominent fashion brands such as Zara and H&M have faced backlash for using indigenous or tribal textile patters and designs that are culturally specific and for which they neither give credit nor pay anything to the cultures that created them. Pop culture celebrities such as Kim Kardashian are often accused of appropriating black culture for braiding their hair in cornrows and excessively darkening their skin in edited photographs. Kardashian's infamous cover of Paper magazine, in which a Champagne glass stands upright on the top of her voluminous glutes has been read by many cultural critics as reperforming representations of curvy black women's figures in the tradition of Sarah Baartman, an African woman of the Khoikhoi tribe who in the nineteenth century was paraded and displayed as a curiosity all over Europe due to her body proportions. What is common to all cases mentioned on the previous page is that it is invariably white people and white culture who appropriate or perform stereotypical representations of other identities, reperforming histories of racism and colonization. However, the debates about cultural appropriation often seem to go nowhere because appealing to a culture's essence is a problem in itself. Cultures are not pure or static, but constantly performed, evolving from contact and exchange in which symbols, behaviours, gestures, customs, cultural artefacts, etc. are adopted from one culture into another. Many people fear that debates about cultural appropriation often foreclose the possibilities of exchange and that they misrepresent cultures as fixed and ossified. On the opposite end of that position, others argue that just because cultural contact is inevitable, it does not mean it is always a fair exchange for all the parties involved, or that it is acceptable for one culture to profit from the artefacts, symbols or performances taken from other cultures under the guise of cultural exchange.

Issues of authenticity and appropriation get all the more complicated in contemporary society because contemporary capitalism thrives on the commodification of everything material and immaterial, including identities and cultures. Performance is a prime vector in this process of commodification, yet very rarely benefits those at the bottom of the economic structure. Art historian Lisa Collins has argued that we should think about this process as 'economies of the flesh', which are the contemporary legacies of the trans-Atlantic slave trade. Economies of the flesh explain why black bodies enter public culture as flesh to be sold, an object to be consumed or a series of performances that can be stripped away from black bodies and re-performed at will. Beyond blackness, the commodification of non-Western cultures and minoritarian identities is ubiquitous in contemporary capitalism. In being commodified and circulated as objects and 'trends', cultures and identities are flattened into stereotypes and misrepresented, a process that solidifies the impression that whiteness is neutral, unmarked and therefore non-performative.

While this chapter has explored how minoritarian subjects strategically use performance to counter negative representations and dominant modes of visuality, the next chapter will explore how performance is used for political activist purposes.

FURTHER READING

Chambers-Letson, Joshua. *After the Party: A Manifesto for Queer of Color Life*. New York: New York University Press, 2018.

Johnson, E. Patrick, and Mae Henderson. *Black Queer Studies: A Critical Anthology*. Durham: Duke University Press, 2005.

Kuppers, Petra. *Disability and Contemporary Performance: Bodies on Edge*. New York: Routledge, 2003.

Perkins, Kathy A., Sandra L. Richards, Renee Alexander Craft and Thomas DeFrantz. *The Routledge Companion to African American Theatre and Performance*. Routledge Theatre and Performance Companions. Abingdon; New York: Routledge, 2019.

Teves, Stephanie Nohelani. *Defiant Indigeneity: The Politics of Hawaiian Performance*. Chapel Hill: University of North Carolina Press, 2018.

5

PERFORMANCE ACTIVISM

PERFORMANCE AS ACTIVISM

In September of 2014, Emma Sulkowicz, a student at Columbia University in New York City started carrying a twin-size mattress everywhere they went on campus, even taking it into class buildings and dorms. Sulkowicz's performance, 'Mattress Performance (Carry That Weight)', was part of their senior art thesis and a way to protest the university's handling of their sexual assault case. In 2012, Sulkowicz had been sexually assaulted in their dorm by a fellow student, and upon complaining to the University, was told that the alleged perpetrator would face no consequences due to lack of evidence. Sulkowicz's durational performance entailed certain self-imposed rules, such as carrying the mattress every time they were on university premises until the student accused of assaulting them was no longer on campus, and not asking for help to carry the mattress but accepting it if people offered. During the eight months in which the performance took place, students would often help Sulkowicz carry the fifty-pound mattress, easing their burden in both literal and symbolic ways by showing support for their cause. Sulkowicz walked the stage with the mattress at their graduation ceremony in May of 2015, despite university officials' repeated attempts to make them desist.

'Mattress Performance (Carry That Weight)' received widespread international media attention, making Emma Sulkowicz the face of a broader movement to address the widespread prevalence of sexual assault on college campuses. In fact, the performance spread in ways

DOI: 10.4324/9780429286377-6

Sulkowicz could not have predicted when student organizations both at Columbia and other colleges around the US declared a 'Carry That Weight' day in October of 2014 and started carrying mattresses in support of survivors of sexual assault. These performances and their circulation through media were part of a broader cultural shift to raise awareness about the pervasiveness of sexual assault in society, which would later coalesce in the #metoo movement. Sulkowicz's example shows us that while one individual's particular instance of activist performance might not by itself bring massive change in society, it can certainly provoke awareness, inspire others to join and contribute to a cascade movement that eventually achieves social change. As the multiplication of 'mattress performances' made manifest, in contemporary society, performance and political action are often inseparable. This happens in part because performance is a powerful instrument to create and circulate symbols under which people can coalesce, and in part because public discourse in our highly mediatized society feeds on images, symbols and various forms of performance.

This chapter explores the connections between performance and political activism. In many of the examples discussed in this chapter, the differences between activism and performance will not be clear-cut. When activism turns into performance or performance is mobilized for activist agendas, some people feel uneasy. This uneasiness comes from the suspicion that mixing performance with activism somehow contaminates the latter, or it makes it less authentic. For these people, performance as an artistic practice that can stir powerful emotions hinders the supposedly rational thinking processes that should define political activism. This kind of critique betrays not only the anti-theatrical prejudice that we have mentioned at several points throughout the book, but also a bias according to which emotions cannot have a valid place in political organizing. Rather than seeing the contemporary blurry limits of performance and activism as a problem, performance studies embraces what the blurriness teaches us about both performance and activism.

To return to the example that opens this chapter: was Emma Sulkowicz's mattress performance any less effective because it was a requirement that they had to fulfil as part of their degree? In other words, was it any less legitimate as a form of protest because it was an art project? What would have a less 'artsy' form of activism looked like for Sulkowicz, and could it have been equally effective?

Is performance supposed to remain separated from life in order to retain its artistic value? The field of performance studies explicitly rejects the perspective that performance and activism should remain separate. Diverging from discourses of conceptual purity that posit a separation between political life and performance, performance studies advocates for mobilizing performance to make social change. It also advocates for evaluating the intention, execution and effects of activist performances before dismissing their political efficacy. Just like any other communicative act, an activist performance will be more effective in achieving its goals when it finds the right audience. And just like many examples of performance art, an activist action might be more effective when it prompts people to question the very frame through which they interpret reality.

WHAT EXACTLY IS PERFORMANCE ACTIVISM?

Activities that we think of as 'performance' and activities that we think of as 'activism' can converge in a variety of ways. For the sake of clarity, this section sheds light on what exactly we talk about when we use the term 'performance activism'. The term activism usually refers to activities that people undertake that are animated by the desire to change some aspect of the status quo that they deem unjust. Activism can take many forms, from canvassing or volunteering for a political campaign to hunger strikes, from sending petitions to elected officials to organizing protests and demonstrations, from online organizing to occupations of public or private property. Based on the broad definitions of performance adopted in this book, all forms of activism can be studied *as* performance, regardless of whether the people carrying out these activist actions understand them from a performance lens. As performance, all forms of activism involve embodied practices that people undertake with the intention of reaching certain audiences for specific purposes, whether this means garnering support to change particular injustices, building or strengthening communities, developing collective strategies for long term social change, or simply having their voices and experiences heard. Even though the stakes of signing a petition and going on a hunger strike are vastly different, ultimately both instances entail a series of embodied behaviours oriented towards prompting changes that will have a certain effect in the world.

That being said, while all forms of activism can be studied as performances, this chapter pays particular attention to those forms of activism that explicitly mobilize symbolic and aesthetic elements as essential instruments in the pursuit of their goals. This means that the chapter will give preference to collective forms of action over individual ones, as well as actions that take place in public view over those carried out in private. Protests and demonstrations that include chanting, singing, dancing, drumming, reading poetry or lying on the street and playing dead are spotlighted in this chapter over activities such as sending petitions, even though arguably the latter is as much a form activism and an example of performance as the former. To be clear, this explicit focus on physical collective action as performance does not seek to diminish the fact that often the most successful forms of activism are those that adopt many different strategies simultaneously and in which collective embodied performances carried out in public work alongside less spectacular forms of action, such as signing petitions, sending emails and volunteering to make phone calls. Performance activism from the perspective of embodied collective action can take on many different forms. Protests, rallies, marches, vigils, funerals, parades, concerts, clowning and puppet shows are only some of these forms.

Sometimes, performance activism takes the form of a framed event, such as the first Slut Walk organized to protest rape culture in Toronto in 2011, or a group of animal rights activists covering their naked bodies in red paint and disrupting a fashion show that showcases fur designs. Other times, performance activism blends into everyday life, like Emma Sulkowicz's mattress performance, or the London group of squatters Autonomous Nation of Anarchist Libertarians, or ANAL, as they prefer to be called, who in 2017 occupied a £15 million mansion belonging to a Russian oligarch in the exclusive district of Belgravia and proceeded to feed the homeless and organize movie nights and talks about gentrification. In the latter cases, it becomes hard to pinpoint exactly when performance activism stopped being an event and became just an unusual mode of living.

The success of activist performances does not depend on how elaborate they are, but on how well they manage to create or use certain symbols in order to convey a message that appeals to and impacts hearts and minds. As we will see in the examples provided in the next section, some of the most successful forms of performance activism do not only bring attention to the ways in which the status quo does not work, but also manage to convey a vision of a better future for the world to see.

A BRIEF (AND INCOMPLETE) HISTORY OF PERFORMANCE ACTIVISM

Although the strategic use of performance and artistic practices became strongly associated with political activism in the second half of the twentieth century, this association has significant historical precedents. In early twentieth-century Russia, for instance, *agitprop* theatre troupes toured the country reaching remote rural regions inhabited by a mostly illiterate population to perform short plays, satires and street theatre skits in order to garner mass support for the revolutionary cause of the workers movement. From Russia, the *agitprop* genre spread to other places in Europe and the Americas in the 1920s and 1930s through the Workers Theatre Movement. This was an international network of theatre groups who made performances in support of diverse working-class struggles, such as unions, strikes and boycotts. As a form of activist performance, *agitprop* aimed to gain allies for particular political causes by boiling these causes down into simplified plots with archetypal characters. This allowed the political messages to be quickly delivered and easily understood, and the skits to travel to a variety of locations with limited production requirements. This ability to distil complex social issues into succinct and impactful messages, create powerful symbols, adapt to shifting circumstances, and savvily do the most with limited resources has characterized many instances of performance activism ever since. This section presents some key moments in the history of performance activism by discussing a few of the world-changing social movements that successfully employed performance to achieve their political goals. For obvious reasons, presenting a comprehensive history of performance activism is beyond the scope of this chapter. The examples discussed in this section, however, demonstrate that in the last decades of the twentieth century and the beginning of the twenty-first, significant social changes have taken place that make it almost impossible to understand contemporary social movements and political mobilization without looking at performance.

The Civil Rights movement in the mid-twentieth-century United States pioneered the strategic use of diverse performance practices in the service of political struggle. The movement explicitly adopted diverse performance techniques to train activists and prepare them for the physical confrontations they would face in fighting the police and angry white mobs. Chief among these techniques were rehearsals and role-playing, which prepared African American activists and their white allies for responding in a non-violent way during street demonstrations, marches and sit-ins at whites-only businesses. During preparatory rehearsals, some activists embodied racist mobs while others role-played as themselves. The former group would verbally and physically attack the latter, presenting them with an opportunity for methodically and repeatedly *rehearsing* what to do in such circumstances. Armed with a repertoire of anti-violence strategies, the activists could face verbal and physical assault with a certain degree of preparation and calmness. Moreover, by performing non-violence in the face of the brutality of racist mobs, the movement rendered the injustice of segregation all the more obvious for the world to see. Activists in the Civil Rights movement were successful because they dramatized their oppression and the injustice of segregation, anticipating the role their enemies would play in the drama and planning accordingly. The images of peaceful black activists and their allies being assaulted by white southerners reached the attention and cultivated the empathy of audiences across the United States and beyond. Once international audiences had seen black activists being brutalized, it became clear that, if the United States wanted to keep its credibility as a world leader, it had to tackle its segregation problem.

The Civil Rights strategy provides fundamental lessons in the use of performance for activist purposes. Its success was a combination of many factors, including the Cold War global order and the United States' need to present itself as a beacon of freedom in opposition to the USSR. However, the use of performance strategies cannot be discounted as a direct contribution to the movement's success. Whereas *agitprop* had literally used short plays to raise working class consciousness, the Civil Rights movement took performance out of its limits as a staged event and smartly incorporated it as a tool for real life action. Rehearsal and role-playing became important activities with the highest stakes, as they could help in keeping activists safe and calm during very volatile and violent situations. Even more importantly, the Civil Rights movement activists understood how to foreground their struggle in ways that fit a dramatic structure for the widest possible audience. This dramatic structure had heroic figures and cruel oppressors, epic battles, beautiful moments of resistance and powerful symbols. In many ways, the Civil Rights movement set the stage for weaponizing performance in political struggles in enduring ways.

In the last few decades of the twentieth century, the ubiquity of television images made it all the more important for activist movements to be mindful of how they were being portrayed in the media. Twenty-four-hour news cycles, the beginnings of the internet, easier access to recording technology and the proliferation of images in society at large provided activists with explicit opportunities to make their causes known to increasing numbers of people. The ubiquity of media, however, also brought about the risk of having their causes disappear amidst an avalanche of information in which public attention shifts quickly between topics. At the end of the twentieth century, political activists who wanted sustained public attention and to make an impact had to become increasingly intentional in their public performances. Social movements such as ACT UP in the United States or the Zapatistas insurgency in Chiapas, Mexico, are excellent examples of the savvy uses of performance that grassroots political struggles adopted at the end of the millennium. Like the Civil Rights movement before them, ACT UP and the Zapatistas understood the power of symbolic communication through embodied actions, carefully prepared public events and strategic use of media to appeal to a worldwide audience.

ACT UP, or the AIDS Coalition to Unleash Power, was founded in New York City in 1987, and had at its peak about 130 branches all over the United States and the world. Still active today, the organization became particularly important in the late 1980s and early 90s for its work in raising awareness about the HIV epidemic, addressing specifically the high cost of treatments and their lack of availability. ACT UP targeted pharmaceutical companies and governmental organizations, such as the Food and Drug Administration and Center for Disease Control. In one of their initial and most famous events in March of 1987, ACT UP activists protested Burroughs Wellcome, the pharmaceutical manufacturer of AZT, which was at that time the only drug available for HIV treatment. Chaining themselves to the balcony inside the New York Stock Exchange and dropping fake dollar bills onto the trading floor, ACT UP activists were calling attention to the high profit the pharmaceutical company was making by selling the drug at a price that almost no HIV-positive person could afford. The attention garnered by their performance had a positive effect and a few days later Burroughs Wellcome lowered the price of the drug by more than thirty percent.

Other ACT UP political actions were perhaps not as easily measurable in their immediate effects, and yet they were even more powerful as performances. In October of 1992, ACT UP held its first 'political funeral' in Washington DC, where members of the movement marched from the Capitol to the White House and scattered the ashes of loved ones who had passed from AIDS-related complications on the White House lawn. Political funerals became a major form of performance activism for ACT UP, making visible that people were dying due to the government's negligence in fighting the epidemic and widespread homophobia. Through a conscious choice to make their grief public and visible, ACT UP activists were employing an emotional political weapon. People would gather to mourn collectively by chanting, giving speeches, crying and holding space for each other's heartbreak. The performative effect of these public funerals cannot be understated. Because grief over a loved one's death is one of the most universal human experiences, public mourning started to make relatable for a lot of people deaths that in public discourse had been previously deemed marginal and associated with the stigma of HIV and non-normative sexuality. By organizing all kinds of performative interventions, ACT UP was essential in pushing government agencies to adopt policies for HIV prevention and treatment.

Another successful example of political action that greatly expanded the possibilities of contemporary performance activism was the Zapatista uprising in 1994 and the subsequent establishment of the Zapatista territory in the Mexican region of Chiapas. The uprising emerged after the implementation of the NAFTA agreement between the United States and Mexico, which opened the door to the privatization of indigenous land that had been formerly protected by the Mexican constitution. After a few weeks of armed insurgency in which the Zapatista Army of National Liberation fought against the Mexican army, gaining control of several towns in Chiapas, the Zapatistas opted for a more sustainable model to create long-term social change in their territory. Basing their way of life on traditional Mayan beliefs and an anti-capitalist perspective, they continue to advocate for sustainable and not-for-profit use of natural resources, such as land and water. Their communities respond to non-hierarchical forms of organization in which decisions are made collectively and indigenous women play a significant role as community leaders in the local government councils. Despite repeated attack by the Mexican government, the army and other paramilitary groups, the Zapatista communities have maintained their independence for over two decades.

The endurance of the Zapatista project and its control of its territory is remarkable, especially when compared to similar indigenous guerrilla movements in other Latin American countries which have been crushed and decimated by the governments they were rising against. Its success cannot be explained in terms of military strategy, since the Zapatistas are greatly outnumbered by and cannot match the resources of the Mexican army. Since the beginning, the insurgency found overwhelming support amongst the indigenous population of Chiapas and demonstrated incredible skill in the use of performative strategies to appeal to a national and international global audience. Using poetry, songs, political statements, speeches, art, murals, a variety of media and the internet, and by organizing events such as marches, land occupations, international *encuentros* of activists and online campaigns, the Zapatistas have successfully presented their struggle as a project for a better and more sustainable world, one based on indigenous values and contrary to capitalist and colonial values. On and offline, their communication strategies, events and appearances are skilful performances that blend together symbols from Mayan indigenous culture, contemporary popular culture and Mexican revolutionary history through figures such as Emiliano Zapata, from whom they take their name. Their performances simultaneously appeal to a global left-leaning civil society and to the indigenous populations that have built their identity in a five-hundred-year-old process of resistance to colonial conquest.

Chief amongst their performative strategies is the Zapatistas performative use of language. From their initial radio broadcast in the beginning of insurgency in 1995 in which they claimed, 'We have a

name, now we will not die!' to the many 're-namings' of the guerrilla leader Galeano, previously known as Subcomandante Marcos,
and before that, as Zacarias, the Zapatista understanding of 'how to
do things with words' would put J. L. Austin to shame. The successive re-namings of the Subcomandante serves to underline the message that their insurgency is not about individual heroes but about
a collective community that is capable of reproducing itself even if
individual people are removed or killed. This dimension of collectiv-
ity is underlined by their use of ski masks when appearing in public.
The ski masks not only provide anonymity, but they make every
communiqué appear as though uttered by the collective voice of the
community, almost as if masked faces were interchangeable. The use
of masking also draws on the longstanding Mesoamerican tradition
of using ceremonial masks in rituals, often to mark transitions and
transformations between the world of the dead and that of the living.
Like war paint that prepares warriors for battle, putting on the ski
masks can be understood as the very ritual performance that makes
an individual into a Zapatista insurgent. Foregrounding the symbols
that strengthen indigenous identity within their communities while
projecting the image of a legitimate liberation struggle for the world
to see, the Zapatistas have created performative strategies of political
mobilization that have influenced social movements ever since.

In the first few decades of the twenty-first century, social movements all over the world have shown increased awareness of how
being intentional about their performances can make or break their
public support – so much so that we can argue that contemporary
social mobilization happens primarily through performative means.
To assert that contemporary activism is performative is not an evaluation of its authenticity. Unlike people who see a problem in activist
agendas that consciously seek media and public attention, a performance studies perspective understands that in a world dominated by
performance, one has to be aware and intentional about performing.
Contemporary movements, such as Black Lives Matter, the Standing
Rock protests against the construction of Dakota Access Pipeline on
indigenous land, and widespread feminist mobilizations in Spanish-
speaking countries, among others, constitute excellent examples of
forms of activism that strategically use performance interventions
to solidify a sense of community, appeal to broad constituencies and
make messages spread quickly around the world.

In the United States, Black Lives Matter has proudly built on the legacy of the Civil Rights movement, while also expanding its range of performative practices. Unlike the Civil Rights movement, which relied heavily on the presence of prominent black men as identifiable leading figures, Black Lives Matter has opted for a horizontal and collective structure that centres the experiences of black femme, queer, trans, and disabled people. The movement, which took its name from a Twitter hashtag, emerged in 2013 from the protests that followed George Zimmerman's acquittal in the murder of African American teenager Trayvon Martin. Like the Civil Rights movement, Black Lives Matter successfully brings to a larger audience of non-black people the injustice experienced by African Americans, especially as it pertains to police violence. Black Lives Matter performances have called attention to the fact that violence against and murder of black people is ubiquitous in the United States. Choreographed die-ins, in which participants lie on the ground and perform being dead, have been a staple of BLM protests since their beginning. The movement has also dramatized specific gestures for their symbolism, such as the 'hands up, don't shoot!' gesture attributed to Michael Brown before being murdered in Ferguson in August 2014. Similarly, the 'Say her name' campaign seeks to change public perception that it is predominantly black males who are victims of police violence by highlighting the ways in which black women are particularly susceptible to the violence of the state and the police force. Through their protest performances, Black Lives Matter has even succeeded in bringing into public debate issues previously considered unrealistic and utopian, such as police and prison abolition.

The Standing Rock Sioux Reservation protests against the construction of the Dakota Access Pipeline on indigenous land, which emerged in April of 2016 and continued until the construction of the pipeline in early 2017, constitute another salient contemporary example of performance activism. Indigenous water protectors and their allies camped for months at the Standing Rock Reservation against an oil pipeline projected to cross through sacred Lakota burial land and in close proximity to natural water resources from which the Lakota people obtain their drinking water and which the pipeline endangered. At the highest peak, the gathering brought together thousands of people, including representatives of hundreds of indigenous tribes across North America, environmental activists, Black

Lives Matter activists, and a group of US Army veterans who volunteered to become a human shield between the water protectors and the police forces. During several months, the camp was the site of an abundance of ritual performances based on Native American cultural traditions, such as prayer gatherings, water chants, dance, drumming and nightly sweat lodges. At the camp site, these ritual performances became political actions through which water protectors showed the sacred connections between the natural environment and native spiritual practices. Like the Zapatistas had done starting two decades earlier, the Standing Rock water protectors used performance to draw from past indigenous traditions and longstanding forms of indigenous resistance against the capitalist exploitation of natural resources, while connecting those traditions with present political struggles and articulating projects for a sustainable future.

In the last few years, widespread feminist mobilizations around the world, but especially in Spanish-speaking countries, have used creative performance interventions that have allowed them to appeal to broad national and international audiences, and virally spread their messages. For example, the song 'Un Violador en tu Camino' (translated in English as 'A Rapist in Your Path', and sometimes adapted under the title 'The Rapist is You!') was created by a feminist collective in Chile for the International Day for the Elimination of Violence against Women in 2019. Synchronizing their movements, women in the collective sang and danced to the lyrics in a public performance that went viral. The lyrics of the song denounce patriarchal state structures, such as courts and the police, for failing to prosecute violence against women, if not directly infringing violence. From Chile, the song travelled to other countries in Latin America and around the globe, eventually being performed in public by groups of women in a variety of countries such as Turkey, India, Lebanon and Kenya. A quick search on YouTube shows a plethora of adaptations of 'A Rapist in Your Path' performed by women in marches and demonstrations all over the world. The speed with which the song spread, being translated and adapted to so many specific cultural contexts is arguably a combination between the possibilities offered by contemporary global internet connection and the power of the original song to synthesize the experience of being subjected to the violence of patriarchy in a way that resonates universally despite local particularities.

All the performance activist examples that we have discussed in this chapter also encountered resistance and detractors: states and corporations who pushed back, police forces that exerted violence and made arrests, and the indifference and criticism of people who do not agree with the activist agenda or who dismiss performance activism as gimmicky and attention-seeking behaviour. Just because performance has the ability to move hearts and minds, it does not mean that it can magically change the opinion of the factions that oppose an activist movement in the first place. What performance can do for an activist movement – quite successfully – is put a movement in the spotlight of public attention, raise awareness about the problems the activists are facing, create a sense of urgency about the issue at hand, change the narrative that media, states, and corporations will push to discredit activists, appeal to those who are sympathetic with the activists to persuade them to show up and do more, and serve as a lever that tilts public opinion in ways that influence policy.

WHEN PERFORMANCE ACTIVISM BACKFIRES

A common criticism of performance activism is that spectacle might detract from the seriousness of the political situation that is being fought for. Perhaps a more nuanced way to think about this issue is that when it comes to using performance to advance activist agendas nothing is unquestionably good or bad, but it can be more or less effective in achieving its goals. Insofar as performance is a tool alongside others in the toolkit that activists may use, it is open to being critiqued and improved. Therefore, perhaps a few paragraphs on how performance activism can be problematic are necessary here. Scholars, activists and artists who participate in and study performance activism can benefit from keeping these caveats in mind.

First, it is helpful to keep in mind that even performance activists animated by the most laudable intentions to achieve positive social change might have blind spots that prevent them from seeing how they are also complicit with certain forms of oppression. Debates about the feminist activist group FEMEN illustrate this point. FEMEN members are famous for their topless impromptu performances at official events and in front of world leaders such as Vladimir Putin. They are also known for their stance against all religions, which they consider to be complicit with patriarchy. FEMEN critics have pointed out that this absolute anti-religious stance and statements made by some group members, such as 'it's better to be naked than in a burka', are not only Islamophobic, but also dismiss and devalue struggles for women's rights that come from non-Western cultures. Within non-Western cultural contexts, many women who voluntarily or involuntarily cover their faces for religious reasons are also struggling for women liberation with strategies that target their particular circumstances. By dismissing these struggles, groups such as FEMEN imply that their model is the only or the superior path to women's liberation. Moreover, nude-bombing public events cannot work all across the world, especially in cases in which women would risk murder or execution. Even with some of their members being incarcerated in Russia, FEMEN members are mostly able-bodied white women whose lives are not seriously threatened by their nude activist performances. The controversy around FEMEN illustrates that when performance is taken up in the name of activism it does not resolve the complexities, contradictions and tensions that are already present within activist movements, but might rather amplify them and bring them to the fore.

The second caveat is related to the first, as often a significant blind spot in discussions of performance activism has to do with privileging forms of public intervention that are based on physical presence and unrestricted access to public space. Public space, however, is neither neutral nor universally accessible, but rather determined by the possibilities of appearance afforded to different bodies in relationship to class, race, gender, ability, etc. Even public spaces that used to be open and accessible for a majority of people are rapidly shrinking in global cities due to developments of contemporary capitalism such as privatization, corporatization and surveillance. This is why, for example, many big cities adopt sanitation and beautification projects that forcefully remove homeless people from certain public locations without offering them any housing alternatives. Not everyone can adopt a politics of presence in performance activism, deciding when and where to appear, congregate and take up space to make political demands. When we talk about, study or organize particular instances of performance activism that are meant to happen in public space, we need to be critical of who is allowed to appear and whose presence is not welcomed, derided, labelled as disruptive or undesirable, or directly banned. For example, a demonstration for labour rights in which the majority of those present are male might make a woman uncomfortable even when she agrees with their political demands, because deciding to enter the crowd might make her subject to harassment and unsolicited physical contact. A majority-white feminist movement such as FEMEN might make women of colour feel unrepresented when not directly dismissed or unwelcome. And plenty of activist performances that call for 'taking up the streets' presume an able-bodied attendance of people who could comfortably sit-in, walk, march or run from the police should they need to. Those who choose forms of performance activism that demand their physical presence in public space put their bodies on the line, often making themselves vulnerable to repression and violence. Even as they do so, they might reproduce normative ways of being in public space that are simply not available to others. This is not a tension to be resolved but rather constantly negotiated. A performance studies perspective, with its focus on the body, can illuminate ways of making activist movements more open and inclusive.

The third caveat in discussions of how performance activism might backfire is that the creative use of performance in service of political projects is not the exclusive patrimony of those who fight for equality and freedom. Performance can be harnessed with great success by bigoted and oppressive groups. In the last decade, we have seen the proliferation of right-wing movements that take up online and offline space to rally people up for their political projects. The white supremacist demonstrators that marched carrying torches in Charlottesville, Virginia, in August of 2017, or the Trump supporters that attempted to take the United States Capitol in January 2021 to overturn the results of the 2020 American presidential election are two good examples of organized crowds that use powerful symbols to garner support for collective political projects – albeit for all the wrong reasons. This is a topic that has not yet been fully explored in the field of performance studies, perhaps because it upsets those who understand the potential of performance to create powerful collective moments and bring about social change. Performance studies scholars tend to easily label protest movements that congregate under progressive principles as 'performance activism', but would be far more resistant to recognize that protest movements with conservative, if not outright fascist, principles work in very similar ways. As we will discuss more in depth in the last chapter of this book, this might be because performance studies as a field tends to celebrate the liberatory power of performance and not so much question how performance has become an operative force of contemporary society. Beyond performance studies as a field, the rising use of performative strategies by contemporary fascist movements brings up very interesting questions for those interested in the potential of performance activism. Can we call these manifestations of grassroots fascism performance activism or should we use a different name? How might our definitions of performance change when we take into account the way it is efficiently mobilized for oppressive and hateful projects?

Finally, performance activism often backfires because of poor execution, insufficient planning, and because it becomes a victim of its own clichés, resulting in trite and repetitive events that fail to have an impact. What holds true of any performance created for exclusively artistic purposes also holds true of performance created for activist purposes—a sloppy, stale, overstated or poor-quality performance is more likely to make people cringe than move them to action. This does not mean that successful performance activism is always made by professionals, but that it needs to be intentional, relevant to the activist issue at hand and gripping.

A FEW LESSONS IN PERFORMANCE ACTIVISM

Successful moments of performance activism might seem spontaneous and highly cathartic and, sometimes, they are. A crowd breaking into song or forming a human chain in front of police officers during a demonstration often emerges as a spontaneous action. More often than not, however, successful performance activism that looks spontaneous and runs smoothly is the result of thoughtful preparation and the application of specific embodied techniques. The antiviolence rehearsal workshops of the Civil Right movement, the public appearances of the Zapatistas and the synchronized multitudes of women dancing to 'A Rapist in Your Path' mentioned earlier are all excellent examples of this. In regards to preparation, performance activism is not that different from artistic performances that happen onstage. That is, just like a stage performer who could exceptionally get away with being unprepared only through a combination of experience and luck, occasional activist events that are not fully planned can produce powerful performative moments. However, just like stage performers, activists who use performance are more likely to succeed as a combination of thoughtful preparation and practice.

The need for thoughtful preparation and practice is a precondition for performance activism to succeed, according to performance studies scholar and Rebel Clown Army founder L. M. Bogad. In his book *Tactical Performance: The Theory and Practice of Serious Play,* Bogad shares the practical lessons for performance activism that he teaches in his workshops. Besides planning and preparation, he advises staying specific by making the performance action relate to the issue at hand, trying to anticipate the reactions of one's opponents and plan accordingly, and identifying the weak points of the political system that could give if enough pressure were applied. Bogad also reminds us of the importance of the story and how it is told, as too often those in power, corporations and the media will happily emphasize the least appealing parts of a demonstration or activist event, such as focusing on urban property destroyed in a riot rather than the legitimate social grievances that motivated rioters to take to the streets in the first place. Because how the story is told can make or break popular support for an activist cause, performance is a powerful tool that activists can mobilize in telling their story and providing images or symbols to be captured by and circulated through media. Bogad also emphasizes the importance of knowing the history of past struggles and their tactical performances, so as to build what he calls a 'counter-institutional memory of tactical innovation', which would allow an activist movement to build on strategies that have been proven to work and avoid repeating the mistakes of others.

Successful contemporary performance activism is skilful in taking advantage of both online and offline platforms to articulate its demands. Performance studies scholar Marcela Fuentes defines this phenomenon as 'performance constellations', or the entanglements between street protest and digital technologies that create opportunities for collective activist projects to thrive. Online and offline, performance can navigate through and reach different times and spaces, redefining the possibilities of contemporary activism. Fuentes cites several examples of performance activism from the last two decades that have successfully merged these online and offline forms of action. One of them is the virtual sit-ins organized by the US collective the Electronic Disturbance Theatre (EDT) in 1998 in support of the Zapatista insurgency. Just as real-life sit-ins can disturb traffic and activity, EDT conceptualized a digital instrument that could do this to obstruct the activity of several Mexican government websites. They designed a DDoS action, or Distributed Denial of Service. This is a classic hacking technique in which users accessed a site that then re-directed them to the Mexican government website and created repeated automatic requests to refresh the website until the government server was overwhelmed and could not carry out its usual service. In addition to EDT's action, Fuentes also explores other examples, such as the 2011 Chilean student movement organization of flash-mobs, various activist strategies first implemented during the 2001 Argentinean economic crisis, the 2014 massive mobilization against the disappearance and murder of forty-three Ayotzinapa students in Mexico, and the contemporary women's mobilization for reproductive rights in Argentina. Even though Fuentes' explicit focus is on protest movements happening in Latin America, specifically in Argentina, Mexico and Chile, we can certainly see 'performance constellations' at play in multiple forms of contemporary protest that happen as multiplatform collective action. What seems certain is that contemporary performance activism is more likely to achieve its goals when it strategically uses both digital and real-life, bodies-on-the-line forms of actions. Activist performance constellations make the particular plight of people in one place legible to a global audience, casting it as a local example in a global struggle against the capitalist monetization of life, the destruction of the environment, and the oppression of the colonized under interlocking forms of racist, heteropatriarchal and ableist injustice.

A final and important lesson is that performance activism is more likely to succeed in moving peoples' minds and hearts if it is beautiful. Beauty, in this sense, is nothing like the shallow hierarchies according to which people's value depends on their physical appearance, or the consumption of aesthetically pleasing objects and experiences encouraged by capitalism. Rather, this notion of beauty, as D. Soyini Madison argues, comes from a longstanding philosophical tradition that equates beauty with truth and justice. Madison talks about her experience of directing her students in a staged performance of *Labor Rites* in the months following the 2011 Occupy movement in the United States. The goal of the performance was to prompt a reflection on the ways in which labour orders the world, from the basic fact that all living organisms require of labour to survive, to the ways in which labour structures human existence, imbuing it with both deep fulfilment and incredible suffering. Madison argues than rather than spelling out specific solutions to labour problems, the goal of the performance was to create moments of beauty for both the performers implicated in its production and the audiences receiving it. The notion of beauty that Madison argues for is in the experiences we have when we feel connected to others and the world beyond our narrow personal interests, in the ways we are moved to imagine and long for the end of conditions of oppression. When experienced in performance, this beauty feels simultaneously like a powerful personal experience that cannot be contained in words and an attribute of an event and object outside of us. This is one of the most important things that performance can bring to activism: the possibility of making political struggle beautiful by conveying in images, symbols, gestures, movements, silences, etc. how much more capacious and fulfilling human life could be if it were organized on principles of truth and justice.

FURTHER READING

The following books by performance studies scholars further explore the relationship between performance and activism:

Bogad, L. M. *Tactical Performance: The Theory and Practice of Serious Play*. New York: Routledge, 2016.

Fuentes, Marcela A. *Performance Constellations: Networks of Protest and Activism in Latin America*. Ann Arbor: University of Michigan Press, 2019.

Madison, D. Soyini. *Acts of Activism: Human Rights as Radical Performance*. Cambridge; New York: Cambridge University Press, 2010.

If interested in learning more about freedom struggles such as the ones mentioned throughout this chapter, you could consult the following titles:

Boyd, Andrew, and Dave Oswald Mitchell. *Beautiful Trouble*. New York: OR Books, 2016.

Conant, Jeff. *A Poetics of Resistance: The Revolutionary Public Relations of the Zapatista Insurgency*. Edinburgh; Oakland: AK, 2010.

Davis, Angela. *Freedom Is a Constant Struggle: Ferguson, Palestine, and the Foundations of a Movement*. Chicago: Haymarket Books, 2016.

Khan-Cullors, Patrisse, and Asha Bandele. *When They Call You a Terrorist: A Black Lives Matter Memoir*. 1st edn. New York: St. Martin's Press, 2018.

6

PERFORMANCE RESEARCH METHODS

WHAT ARE RESEARCH METHODS?

Research methods are toolkits for solving a problem through clear and identifiable steps, such as the gathering of information or data, its analysis and the pronouncement of specific conclusions based on that analysis. Performance studies methods are *qualitative* rather than *quantitative*. Research in performance studies does not look at reality as if it were fixed and measurable but rather as phenomena that is subjectively experienced and can be observed and interpreted. The knowledge produced in performance studies can be reported in written text, media or embodied performance. The questions asked depend a lot on the person asking them, the problems that they care about, the domains of social life in which they want to intervene, and their previous experiences and knowledge. There is an almost endless set of questions about the world around us that we can explore through a performance studies lens, but generally speaking performance studies research questions most often focus on the interplay between embodied performance, political economy, social hierarchies, history and identity.

As stated in this book's introduction, in the field of performance studies, performance is simultaneously an object of study, an analytic and a research method. This means that the field studies performances happening in the world, uses performance theory as the foundation to understand how meaning is socially created and transmitted through the body, and employs performance as a methodology of research by both studying life phenomena as performance and creating performances to intervene in social processes.

DOI: 10.4324/9780429286377-7

This chapter discusses some of the most commonly used research methods in performance studies, providing examples of what these methods entail and how they apply to specific case studies. The examples discussed in this chapter are by no means the only ones worth studying nor the only ones that have shaped the field. Because of its interdisciplinary nature, performance studies scholarship and practice can mix several of the methods explained in this chapter. This is because performance studies methods allow us to pick and choose which tool or combination of tools best serves to explore a specific set of questions we have about some aspect of reality. Performance studies methods also borrow elements from different fields of knowledge to look at performances, draw from theory and analyse what performances do in given social contexts. Performance studies scholars are also often practitioners, that is, they make embodied performance to explore their research questions or to report their research findings.

Performance studies methods emerge from a critical perspective. Looking at reality through a critical perspective means that we seek to understand the connections between people's lived experiences and the social structures in which these experiences unfold. It also means that performance studies research projects are animated by a desire to deeply understand the causes of various forms of injustice and correct them. Because of this critical perspective, performance studies methods and theory are intertwined. This does not mean that they are one and the same. While methods are processes to conduct research, theories are sets of evidence-based ideas and discourses that attempt to explain some dimension of reality. Theory and methods are intertwined because they are in constant dialogue, insofar as methods produce new theory or reshape existing theories and theory informs the questions asked in research and the steps taken to answer them.

ARCHIVAL RESEARCH AND PERFORMANCE HISTORIOGRAPHY

As researchers, we are aware of what happened in the past because traces of past events are available to us in documents and archives. Imagine, for instance, that we want to study the period of social upheaval known as the Russian Revolution of 1917. In order to do so, we might turn to history textbooks, which, in turn, are based on documents available from that time such as newspapers, books, legal documents and public statements written by ideologues of the different factions involved. We might also turn to personal memoirs that capture people's recollections, and folk and vernacular expressions, such as songs. However, as mentioned in previous chapters, some very important events in the historical past are not so readily available in documents and traditional archives at all. This is often because the documents that cover these events never existed in the first place, because they were destroyed by human intervention or by accident, or because what is available in these documents is a partial account that leaves out important things. It is not a coincidence that so much has been written about the Russian Revolution of 1917 – a revolution that was successful in overturning a monarchy and creating a socialist state. By the same logic, we have much less recorded data from the European colonial administrations in nineteenth-century Africa and the numerous armed revolutions of the colonized peasantry against the white colonizers. This is not accidental. Although we tend to think about history as an objective truth, history is always an interpretation of the past mediated by the limits and intentions of those who recorded it. Or, as the common saying goes, history is written from the perspective of the victors. This is where a performance studies methodology can be useful. Turning to performance to study the historical past often helps with the limits or shortcomings of historical archives or can at least excavate perspectives about the past that might have remained out of official historical accounts but that have been sometimes successfully transmitted as embodied knowledge.

This section will explore the relationship between archival and historiographic research and performance. But first, what is historiography, and how is it different from history? Historiography literally means *the writing of history*, and it is a self-reflexive term and field of knowledge concerned with the recording and telling of history, that is, the making of historical narratives. Historiography looks beyond the records of what happened to understand how the records of what happened came to be. Conducting historiographic research in performance studies entails looking at embodied performances to understand past phenomena and how these phenomena influence our historical present, and doing so while making transparent the power dynamics at work in producing historical records. This can mean studying the history of particular performance traditions in their social contexts, as one will do to understand, for instance, how the rise of the Nazis in 1930s Germany shaped the lives and artistic practices of Jewish theatre performers, or how the expansion of the British empire in nineteenth-century India changed traditional dance practices to separate performers from audiences. But it also means understanding historical events *as* performance and asking performance-centred questions of history. For example, how might certain performance traditions across the Americas, such as festivals, ceremonies and storytelling, speak of anti-colonial resistance that cannot be found in historical archives? Performance studies scholar Renée Alexander Craft has tackled this question in her study of the Portobelo carnival tradition in Panama. In their carnival performances, the small Afro-Latino community in Portobelo, who call themselves and their carnival tradition 'Congo', commemorate the legacy of African fugitive slaves, while mocking the Spanish crown and the Catholic Church. Alexander Craft's work is an excellent example of how looking at live performances such as carnival can reveal a lot about historical processes that are not recorded in archives. While recognizing the importance of live performance, Alexander Craft has also been working with members of the Portobelo community for years to build a digital archive of the Congo carnival as a project of cultural preservation.

A fundamental advantage of looking at history through performance is that it presents an opportunity to correct the tendency of history to appear to us as a linear narrative. History appears in a linear narrative when we see the past as a sequence of events linked by causal relationships such that the way they developed seems the only possible outcome. This is especially true because Western cultures traditionally understand time as linear progress. However, the relationship of causality that we see in retrospect might not have been there in the first place. Against this linear view, looking at historical events through performance helps us understand them as a push and pull of different social forces, agents and factions in conflict. Full of contradictions and potential, historical events could have developed in different directions and generated different outcomes. If events do not necessarily happen in causal sequence but as a result of the push and pull of social forces, how do we adequately represent the historical past to account for these complexities?

Some performance studies scholars have argued that performance is, in fact, key to representing these complexities. Joseph Roach proposes the term 'surrogation' to characterize the process through which societies remember certain things from their past while forgetting others. For example, during a New Orleans jazz funeral, a community comes together to perform music in the absence of the departed person. The communal performance and the social bonds it generates serve as a surrogation of the departed. Roach thinks that rather than looking for authenticity in performance, we should look at the processes through which some performances are substituted by others in a continuity that might not be readily apparent and yet perpetuates culture. The very concern with performance authenticity is, for Roach, a by-process of surrogation, as the fit of the new performance against the old is never perfect and the process creates anxieties.

Archival and historiographic research in performance studies also present serious challenges. A primary challenge is building connections between pieces of data, particularly filling the gaps to create a coherent narrative while also interrogating why there are data gaps in the first place. The question, then, is not so much whether historical evidence is true or false, but whether it is plausible. When building a narrative from historical evidence, the performance historiography scholar knows that her narratives are not perfect, insofar as they attempt to provide the most plausible interpretation of how things occurred.

Often times, doing archival historical work is also about challenging existing narratives and power structures. With the understanding that narratives are man-made, we can see that those we have inherited about certain events are partial accounts open to revision. As these narratives change, archives might also change to include previously ignored events, people and practices. Historical research also consists of re-writing history, as one seeks to revisit and correct the gaps of existing histories. Sometimes, the historical archives simply do not contain detailed documents that reflect particular peoples or histories. Faced with this problem, the question for the historian becomes what alternative evidence might count. Theatre and performance scholar Harvey Young has turned to the natural landscape paintings of Robert S. Duncanson (1821–1872), a free black painter in Antebellum United States. Duncanson's landscapes transmit claustrophobic emotions, evidence used by Young to argue that the painter's work comments on the feelings of entrapment, the experience of captivity, and the desires for freedom of the black body. As Young's argument demonstrates, performance historiography often consists of asking where certain bodies figure in historical archives, why they are missing from the archives in the first place, and what evidence we can turn to in order to talk about this.

Other times, the challenge for the historian is seeing what the archive contains from a new or different perspective, especially as the development of theory provides critical tools that can explain why certain sets of evidence that have not been in the focus of attention might need to be taken into account. In his book *The Amalgamation Waltz: Race, Performance, and the Ruses of Memory,* performance studies scholar and cultural critic Tavia Nyong'o argues for using the archive as a practice of 'countermemory' precisely by interrogating how, when read against the grain, historical evidence might provide grounds for alternative interpretations of history. In a compelling example of this practice of countermemory, Nyong'o mentions a book in the collection of the Wellcome Library in London. A tag attached to this book states that its cover is made with the skin of the 'Negro whose Execution caused the War of Independence'. This is an alleged reference to Crispus Attucks, an Afro-Native sailor and fugitive slave who was one of the five American civilians killed by British troops in March of 1770 in Boston, in one of the incidents that sparked the American Revolution. The development of genetic testing confirmed a few years ago the tag's claim to be a hoax as the cover is actually made of cow skin. Nyong'o argues that the book is still a valid historical document not because of its authenticity, but because it is a long-time object of fascination. The forgery itself and the legend around it can be the objects of historical analysis and reveal the fascination with the black body that has characterized the history of racial relations in America. In Nyong'o's perspective, 'performative historiography' looks at the historical truths that can be uncovered by such objects, and in doing so it also reveals traditional, empiricist historiography as incomplete or flawed, because it cannot fully account for how the meanings of certain objects circulate in society. But how does one approach the process of making meaning of an object found in the archive or a performance? The next section explores this question.

CLOSE READINGS

Close reading, which was first developed in the study of literature, is a method in which different parts of a written text are closely analysed to understand how they connect to produce meaning. Even though it first started as a method of textual analysis, close reading can also be productively used to look at other cultural products, such as images, film or live performance. In performance studies, doing a close reading implies looking at a performance in detail to analyse its content and structural components, whether the performance in question is a live event, a performance archived in some form of media, or other kinds of objects that in their interaction with particular audiences can be studied as performance. We would ask questions such as: What are the parts of the object or event that allow us to extract meaning from it? How do these different parts relate to each other? Are there specific patterns that we can see, such as repetition, parallels, tensions, or oppositions? Does the object or event we are looking at make reference to other cultural objects or performances? How does it make us feel as a spectator/witness/co-participant? How is it speaking to particular groups rather than a broad universal audience? Can we see connections between the performance and its social, historical or political context? Does the performance illustrate or put into question particular theories about society or the world at large?

In other words, close readings think about the social conditions and effects of performances and ground this thinking in their formal qualities, as well as their conditions of production, and the way they are received and circulated. An important part of this is to consider also how people might look at, understand, experience or participate in a performance given their subjectivity and position within a social hierarchy. Because performance is a social practice, there is simply no such thing as a performance whose meaning will resonate with all people across different geographical locations and historical times. For instance, the fact that in some cultures it is customary to wear black at funerals while in others white is more appropriate exemplifies how the meaning we ascribe to social performances depend on cultural contexts.

Most of the time, we are not aware of how we might get meaning out of the objects, signs, images and performances we see in the world because our brain goes through this process much quicker than we are conscious of. Meaning-making is not only influenced by our personal experiences but also the social context in which our perception has formed. This context, in turn, will be shaped by particular 'commonsense' notions of race, class, gender, sexuality, etc. This is why media representations of people have such a noticeable influence over stereotypes when, for instance, we see more women than men depicted cleaning their house in advertising, or we see Middle Eastern men more often cast in movies as terrorists than doctors, professors or artists. Because meaning is not inherent to objects but is socially produced, when conducting a close reading of a performance, it is crucial that we critically think about how it is produced, shared and received – sometimes in ways of which participants might not be fully aware. We also want to scrutinize our own way of looking at a performance. How might our perception and understanding of a particular performance be influenced by factors such as our age, class, race, methodological or scholarly training, previous knowledge, or expectations? When reporting the results of our close reading, we want to be open in disclosing our positionality so our reader/audience knows what we are basing our analysis on.

To illustrate how a close reading methodology can be applied to the study of performance, let us turn to a practical example. Imagine a performance, such as bullfighting. A cultural tradition in many countries, including Spain, Portugal, France, Mexico, Colombia, Venezuela and Peru, bullfighting is a physical contest in which a man kills a bull according to certain rules and prescriptions. If we were to apply a close reading to a bullfighting event, we might start by looking at its different participants and elements: the bullfighter, the bull, the audiences and the way they are seated, the shape of the arena, the costumes worn by the participants, the movements, the interactions between the bull and the bullfighter. We can go even deeper into our close reading by isolating the different parts of certain actions, for instance looking at the ways in which the torso, head, and gestures of the bullfighter might express aggression, defiance or bravery, or the ways in which the body of the animal might express fear, suffering or hostility. We might choose to include in our close reading other elements around the main event, such as the posters and brochures that advertise it, or the website we browse to buy the tickets. We would ask questions such as: How does the staging of this event create particular narratives of danger, bravery and victorious resolution?

How do these elements contribute to making this performance fit into cultural traditions, expectations of masculine bravado, images of nationalism or ideologies that justify the dominance of man over other animal species?

When we pose these questions, we move from the observation of a particular set of happenings to the drawing of conclusions that contextualize the event in a broader cultural and social context. We might find it helpful to turn to critical theory to understand how the event manifests broader systems of power. When introducing a critical theory perspective, we would look at the event with tools we would borrow from different toolkits, such as feminism, psychoanalysis, critical race theory or eco-critique. Depending on what questions we ask, our interpretations might change. We might also choose to do a close reading of this performance by putting several or all of these theoretical perspectives into dialogue in order to enrich our conclusions. Performance studies is generally interested in situated contexts, which means recognizing that things do not always have the same universal meaning. An ecologically critical spectator who is concerned about the relationship of humankind with nature might be horrified by the killing of an animal for the sake of spectacle, while someone who is attached to masculinist tropes of domination of man over nature might find it beautiful and breath-taking. Moreover, despite associations of bullfighting with traditional models of masculinity and heteropatriarchy in the countries that follow this tradition, the bullfighter's tight attire, revealing the shape of the male body, can also make room for some spectators' queer desires. Ultimately, the elements that make up the performance will be understood in different ways by different participants.

A performance is not an object with fixed meaning, but a cultural process, a site that captures social values, mores, customs and views about the world and its politics, often in conflict with each other. Because meaning is not fixed, there is no absolutely right way of conducting a close reading of performance, but there are many risks of oversimplifying the complexity of these cultural processes. When we apply a close reading methodology to a live performance event, we are venturing into the terrain of ethnographic participant observation, as we will see in the next section.

PERFORMANCE ETHNOGRAPHY

Ethnography is a research methodology that records and interprets human behaviour of particular groups in a given setting. For the researcher, this implies physically encountering the group that they want to study, spending time 'in the field', and participating in the social world of the group. During this time, the ethnographer speaks with people informally or interviews them to learn about the meanings they ascribe to their own behaviours. The goal is to uncover deeper truths beyond just factual information, such as cultural values, symbols, beliefs and in-group hierarchies and power dynamics. In performance studies, ethnography takes performance as both its object of study and its methodology, both documenting actual performances and examining how particular social worlds are shaped through performance. At its core, performance ethnography has a critical and socially engaged agenda. This means that the ethnographer seeks to understand how human actions and experiences are traversed by power structures in the particular setting they study while also paying close attention to how performance might contest those very power structures.

Ethnography as a research method predates performance studies. Emerging and developing alongside colonization, ethnography initially originated as an attempt to study what Western social scientists considered to be 'primitive' peoples. These were often native societies in Africa, Asia, the Americas and Australia who were deemed worthy of study precisely because they were considered radically different from Western civilization. Implicitly, the interest in studying them came from the conviction that they would eventually disappear with the advance of modernity. In the nineteenth and early twentieth centuries, the classical image of an ethnographer was that of a white person – most often a man from a comfortable upbringing – traveling to study natives around the world, and recording their behaviours, first on notepads and then on sound recorders and cameras. These first kinds of ethnographic encounters between Western researchers and non-Western societies helped shaped the racist Western imagination, influencing how Westerners think about certain groups as 'exotic' and fixed in a primitive past.

The rise of anti-colonial critique in the mid-twentieth century put into question Western ways of relating to non-Western people around the world. This development gave rise to a more critical stance towards ethnography within academia. Starting in the 1960s, many social scientists started to pay attention to the ways in which their work was at risk of exoticizing and misrepresenting the people they were studying. Over the last few decades of the twentieth century – and with the hiring of more scholars who tackle issues of race, gender and sexuality – scholarship started to increasingly critique how people belonging to minority categories had been previously represented in the social sciences. This contributed to reassessing the role that ethnography had played in creating racist stereotypes.

In academic settings, performance studies emerged at a time when traditional modes of doing ethnography were being questioned. Thus, ethnographic methods in performance studies tended from the very beginning to be self-critical, a value that has been a constant in the field ever since. This does not mean that critical performance ethnography has always been unbiased or safe from the risks of misrepresenting the people it studied. Rather, it means that the ethnographic perspective in performance studies is based on the understanding that ethnographers operate within power relations and that they have ethical obligations towards their research subjects.

Dwight Conquergood (1949–2004) was a seminal figure in the consolidation of performance studies as academic inquiry from the 1980s onward. While chairing the Department of Performance Studies at Northwestern University, he pushed the boundaries of the field by arguing that ethnographers should not think of themselves simply as participant-observers of the social settings they study but rather 'co-performative witnesses'. Conquergood astutely pointed out that there is no such thing as an ethnographer who can observe a social reality without changing it in some form or other with their very presence. Co-performative witnessing means that by participating in a given social setting, the ethnographer performs for her interlocutors as much as they perform for her. More importantly, witnessing is a disposition that goes well beyond simply observing. An ethnographer that witnesses a set of social struggles against injustice and oppression has the responsibility of doing work that helps and gives voice to those struggles. Conquergood's work helped to transform the field of performance ethnography from a position of observing and studying to one of sharing in ethical responsibility.

At its core, Conquergood's ideas were stating something that might seem quite obvious to performance ethnographers in the present but that a lot of ethnographic research had been ignoring since the first Western anthropologists went to study groups of people around the world: that the way we make meaning of other peoples' behaviours is never neutral, but shaped by our own perceptions and experiences. As a result, objectivity is simply not possible. Rather than striving to be objective, the ethnographer's responsibility is to be rigorous and support their claims through carefully collected data, while revealing what belief systems, knowledges and values they are using to make those claims. The ethical stance for the ethnographer is to be as transparent as possible about how their own personal experiences shape their perspective. This does not mean that the ethnographer denies truth and facts, but rather that they are aware that the account of the field they provide is always partial and incomplete.

Conquergood defined four problematic positions that were to be avoided in the ethnographer's approach of the people they study:

The first position was that of the 'custodian's rip-off'. This would be the position of an ethnographer only driven by self-interest and the success of his own research project who completely disregards the safety, dignity and well-being of his interlocutors. Like a custodian who rips off artefacts from native cultures to display them in a museum out of context, this kind of ethnographer's position is one of exploitation of the people studied. The second position Conquergood deemed undesirable for an ethnographer is that of 'infatuation'. This position is characterized by a romantic and superficial view of the people and circumstances the ethnographer studies, flattening out the interlocutors' experiences under a superficial understanding that 'we are all the same', trivializing the particulars of different cultures, overlooking contradictions and whatever does not fit into the ethnographic account. For Conquergood, this perspective was dangerous because it was shallow. The third problematic position is the 'curator's exhibition', which is just as superficial as infatuation. The 'curator's exhibition' is the position of an ethnographer who is fascinated by cultural differences and who exoticizes everything as primitive and culturally remote. The fourth position is that of the 'sceptic's cop-out', who remains detached from the people he studies and convinced that he cannot possible engage an identity outside of his own in any meaningful or transformative way. Conquergood believed this last position to be the most reprehensible of the four, for while infatuation and superficial understanding of a culture might in time grow into deeper forms of engagement, the sceptic avoids engaging altogether, therefore never allows himself to grow out of his ignorance.

As an alternative to these four positions, Conquergood proposed 'dialogical performance', a position in which the self and other are in dialogue so they can question and challenge one another in ways that might lead to personal growth for everyone involved. Dialogical performance is not just empathy, although it does require high doses of it; it is an open relationship between self and other. It remains open because the people represented in the ethnographic research are not fixed in time but are constantly evolving. From the dialogical performance perspective, the ethnographer understands that the ethnographic account they are providing exists at a particular moment of the ethnographic encounter, a moment that is bound to change. Therefore, the ethnographer should avoid presenting people as if they were stuck in a timeless moment and always the same. At the beginning of this section, we noted that one of the most common and well-deserved critiques of ethnography was that it risked representing non-Western societies as primitive and fixed in the past. This happened precisely because the specificity of a time-bound ethnographic encounter was taken to represent the entirety of a culture. To avoid this tendency is to understand that dialogical performance is not a fixed object but a relationship between the people that participate in it.

D. Soyini Madison, a leading figure in performance ethnography and one of Dwight Conquergood's former students at Northwestern University, argues that the ideals that should guide one's research in the field are kindness, friendship and honesty. In her influential book, *Critical Ethnography: Method, Ethics, and Performance*, Madison argues that it is the ethnographer's obligation to listen with an open heart and attention even when they feel unease or disapproval over what is being said. Madison's prompt seems deceptively simple, and yet it is deeply radical because engaging in dialogue even when we find it difficult to do so demands a lot of critical awareness, self-reflection and vulnerability from the ethnographer. This is because fieldwork is relational. This means that the ethnographic encounter is always a relationship, and it is the ethnographer's responsibility to set the tone for it to be one of mutual exchange and benefit instead of an extractive one.

As a research method, critical ethnography is committed to advocating for and holding space for those in minoritarian positions, those who have been traditionally disempowered and relegated to the margins of society. Critical ethnography aims to help these groups in having their voices and experiences heard and valued, and should also strive to counter misrepresentations that contribute to the disempowerment of certain communities. For example, in his ethnographic study of gay male sex workers in Brazil, *Tourist Attractions,* performance studies scholar Gregory Mitchell purposefully represents his research interlocutors from a perspective that counters medical accounts that depict them as vectors of sexually transmittable diseases and victim narratives that see sex workers as people in need of rescue. Instead, Mitchell paints a complex portrait of sex work at the intersection of interracial desire, tourist economy and sexuality. In his ethnography, sex work is performative labour. Not only because sex workers produce particular emotional responses in clients, but also because of how they perform their masculinity according to expectations of race and class. Their performative labour becomes evident, for instance, when they perform 'butch masculinity' to lure a gay sex tourist who is enchanted by the possibility of having sex with a man that self-defines as heterosexual. Mitchell's ethnography also does justice to the complex economic conditions that structure sex tourism globally by depicting sex work as an activity that is essential to the contemporary tourist industry, while also shaping sexual, racial and class identities for both sex workers and their clients.

In critical ethnography, the experiences of oppressed groups should serve to question the way society is organized as a whole and the power structures that have relegated the minoritarian perspective to the margins in the first place. This means that critical ethnography does not simply include minoritarian voices in existing power arrangements. Rather, in bringing minoritarian voices into the conversation, critical ethnography questions the principles on which existing power arrangements are built in favour of more egalitarian ones. Critical performance ethnography can be a powerful activist tool that the ethnographer uses to advocate for her interlocutors. This does not mean that the ethnographer speaks for or in place of her interlocutors but that she is aware of how her ethnographic work might help their cause and does her best to achieve this.

AUTOETHNOGRAPHY

Autoethnography is a subcategory of ethnography in which the object of study is one's self and personal experiences. We know, however, that the self is always deeply intertwined with others, such that we cannot really make sense of our identities without taking into consideration the environment in which they are shaped. This environment includes our immediate family and friends, who deeply influence our values, worldviews, preferences or political views, and also the social positions we inhabit and/or are afforded to us given our gender, race, class or national belonging. Because we bear the traces of the social forces around us, the study of the self has the potential to reveal a lot about those social forces. When ethnographers look at themselves to understand how they are being shaped by social processes, they are doing autoethnography. In other words, autoethnography is a cultural analysis that starts with one's self in order to say something about society more broadly.

Even though the autoethnographic focus on the self overlaps with other genres such as memoir or autobiographical narratives, autoethnography is different in critical ways. Whereas memoir and autobiography focus primarily on personal experiences for the sake of painting a portrait of a specific person, autoethnography is generally interested in the relationship between the self and the broader cultural and social dynamics in which the self is immersed. Even as it constitutes a source of self-discovery and reflection, rigorous autoethnography avoids narcissistic navel-gazing. In autoethnography, it is not enough to assume that one's experience, as interesting or exceptional as it might be, is inherently enough to constitute relevant scholarship. Rather, personal experiences are analysed from a critical perspective in order to illuminate how power structures shape an individual's life. Beyond the benefits of self-reflection, this constitutes the essential scholarly relevance of autoethnography: in reflecting on the socio-political dimensions of our own personal experience, we offer others the possibility to reflect on theirs, and therefore, we open up a space for collective reckoning and, perhaps, collective solidarity

Within the field of performance studies, autoethnography places performance as the primary object of study in order to understand the self and its relationships with others, as well as what these relationships reveal about power, identity and social struggles. Performance studies scholar Bryant Keith Alexander writes in his book, *Performing Black Masculinity,* about delivering a eulogy at his father's funeral. Starting from this personal experience, he reflects on the broader cultural implications of the eulogy as a performance genre that marks a rite of passage in which a group of people come together to acknowledge someone's passing, celebrate their life, memorialize them and say goodbye. In addition, as a black queer man and university professor, performing the eulogy became an opportunity for Alexander to reflect on his complex relationship with his working-class black father. Alexander's eulogy goes beyond the personal experience of a son mourning his father to reflect on different models of black masculinity, upward mobility, intergenerational conflict and class differences within the black community.

Performance studies scholar Patrick Anderson exemplifies a more recent turn in the field of autoethnography, incorporating a perspective that de-centres the human as the only agent that performs. In his *Autobiography of a Disease,* Anderson writes about his struggle with an antibiotic-resistant bacterial infection that almost killed him. He uses third person accounts of his experience in the hospital combined with first person accounts of the bacteria that infected him. Through engaging and beautiful writing, Anderson uses illness as the subject of research to talk about the different elements that influence a person's recovery, such as interactions with physicians, the caring labour of nurses, and the support of family and friends. He also provides an account of the very material dimensions that can determine one's survival, such as having the kind of insurance that covers long hospitalizations and complicated procedures. Anderson's autoethnography is an account of what illness means simultaneously in someone's personal experience and in the social and economic context in which the ill person lives.

Like the ethnographic study of others, autoethnography should start from carefully crafted research questions and exhaustive research plans. It should also include clear ideas of what data will be used. To return to the examples on this page, Alexander's autoethnography looks at a performance event, the eulogy, and his personal memories of his father, which are collected in artefacts such as photographs. In Anderson's case, the data that he starts from is not as much a framed performance event, but a series of everyday life moments collected through months of a nearly lethal disease that he pieces together from medical records, his own writings while convalescent and his mom's diary of that time. Careful consideration of research questions and data is extremely important because, though highly subjective, autoethnography should still be rigorous.

ORAL HISTORY PERFORMANCE

Oral history is the practice of studying the historical past by interviewing individuals who experienced it personally and can recount historical moments through their own perspective. These interviews are often collected and stored in archives. As a method of inquiry, oral history is a particular subfield of the ethnographic interview used in many fields and disciplines from history and sociology to documentary film and digital storytelling. Because oral history pays attention to individuals' lived experiences, it can potentially introduce into historical accounts the perspectives of people and groups that have been left out or correct the historical account for those whose story has been told by others in partial, incomplete or outright false ways. For example, in the 1930s, a number of independent and government-funded projects in the United States started interviewing and collecting the stories of elder African Americans who had been enslaved. The historical significance of this project was enormous, as it was making accessible on a large scale in written transcriptions and sound recordings the experience of slaves from their own perspective. As mentioned in this book's introduction, it is far from coincidence that those who tend to be left out of historical accounts often have rich oral traditions passed through the generations and in which narrative forms serve, among other purposes, that of constituting a people's collective memory and sense of self. Think for instance about the role that narrative forms such as folktales and myths have in Native American communities, and how the colonial process of so-called 'civilization' consisted of, alongside explicit forms of violence, casting a dismissive light on these narrative forms as subjective, non-factual and therefore not 'objective' historical information. Oral history attempts to correct some of these biases of historical archiving practices by attending to orally transmitted stories.

In addition to being used to record and analyse people's experiences, performance studies oral history is often also used as inspiration for the creation of beautiful, rigorous and politically inspiring performances. Oral history performance is based on the principle that the subjective dimension of the stories people tell adds richness and depth to historical accounts. When people speak about their experiences, whole worlds of meaning are contained in their volume, tone, pitch, rhythm or intonation. The gestural, kinetic, emotional and sensorial dimensions are essential to language and are as important as words in the creation of meaning. Perhaps more than other fields that use oral history, performance studies pays attention to the embodied dimensions of narrative and attempts to capture them in performance. This mode of conducting oral history is based on the assumption that personal narratives cannot be separated from their performance, and vice versa – that performance is a particularly suited medium to capture and transmit personal narratives in their full richness.

Oral history performance has the explicit purpose of empowering individuals or social groups whose stories are not told or are misrepresented, and this purpose often guides the process of conducting and staging oral histories. In its politically engaged orientation, oral history performance is neither purely factual nor fictional but exceeds these categories. In fact, oral history performance complicates traditional ways of thinking about facts and fiction as mutually exclusive categories. Instead of choosing either pole of this opposition, oral history performance presents the ways in which historical forces shape people's experiences, and how they are understood through particular subjectivities. Performance studies scholar E. Patrick Johnson's book *Sweet Tea: Black Gay Men of the South* tells the stories of several black gay men and their personal experiences growing up in the US South, navigating their racial and sexual differences in a wide range of family, church, work and social settings. Johnson's book also became a staged performance (and more recently a documentary film) with several iterations in which Johnson embodied the stories of his interlocutors alongside his own and toured all over the country for years. Watching Johnson's performances is a beautiful, compelling testament to what oral history performance can achieve. His oral history methodology is not an investment in the truth, but in validating the narrator's experience and subjectivity, that is, what the narrator remembers and values from their own stories. The performance also complicates stereotypes and one-dimensional expectations regarding black respectability, Southern conservative values and homophobia, in order to paint a complex, often beautiful, and sometimes heart-breaking corollary of experiences. A few years after the publication of *Sweet Tea*, Johnson published *Honeypot: Black Southern Women Who Love Women*, collecting the stories of black, same-sex-loving women from the South. Both projects purposely resist offering a traditional scholarly analysis of people's narratives, instead letting these narratives stand for themselves as what Johnson calls 'quotidian forms of theorizing'.

Sometimes, oral history performance is used to illuminate the complexity of political, social or intercultural conflicts by depicting the everyday personal experiences of those involved in them. In doing so, oral history performance serves to capture historical events in ways that other available mediums, such as journalism or traditional history, cannot. Ana Deveare Smith's critically acclaimed one-person plays *Fires in the Mirror* and *Twilight* are prime examples of this oral history technique. *Fires in the Mirror* focuses on the conflicts between the black and Hasidic Jewish populations in the Crown Heights neighbourhood of Brooklyn in the early 1990s. The neighbourhood had been the setting of violent riots, which originated with a car accident in which a Hasidic man killed a black child, followed by the killing of a Jewish man by a group of black youth. *Twilight* focuses on the 1991 fatal beating of Rodney King by police officers in Los Angeles, the acquittal of the responsible officers in trial, and the ensuing riots. For both pieces, Deveare Smith conducted dozens of interviews with residents, community leaders, politicians and people who had directly participated or were affected by the riots. In the plays, she performs as her interlocutors, presenting the many different personal experiences and factions in opposition while avoiding to judge or offer her perspective on them. Deveare Smith's work is an example of oral history performance that strives to present oral history with as much fidelity to the real events as possible.

This, however, is not the only way of staging oral history performance. Often, the staging of oral history is accompanied by observations and analysis from the researcher. This has the goal of deepening engagement with what is being narrated and of opening up the subtext embedded in personal narratives. In one of the seminal oral history books in performance studies, *Telling Bodies Performing Birth*, Della Pollock collected oral histories of child birth to offer an analysis of how notions of pain, motherhood and women's bodies are produced in these personal stories. She also showed that in child birth these personal stories always intersect with medical and cultural discourses, gender roles and personal expectations. When adding a layer of analysis to oral history narratives, the researcher does not fabricate the narratives, but simply excavates meanings that are already contained below its surface. Whether the researcher only presents the oral histories as collected or adds her analysis, it is important to remember that the primary purpose of oral history performance is to do justice to the complexity of the story, not to transform or obscure it.

We might feel tempted to question what is the value of oral history performance as a mode of preservation of personal narratives in an age in which technological advancement allows us to easily record, preserve and access first-hand the voices, memories and gestures of folks as they perform their own stories. What could a scholar/performer add to this? Perhaps it is useful to think about this as the difference between photography and painting. The invention of photography did not eliminate painting but liberated it from having to copy reality, allowing it instead to explore many other creative dimensions. Similarly, the potential of oral history performance is not only the collection and preservation of personal narratives, nor is it a nostalgic appreciation of live performance against technological mediation. Rather, its importance lies in its potential to be a transformative experience for all parties involved. This transformative experience consists of being allowed an entrance into someone's story through mutual vulnerability and witnessing, and holding the space for them to tell it. This might seem a rather simple and modest goal, and yet holding place for people to tell their stories or attempting to retell their stories in performance from a place of respect and understanding are some of the most radical political acts.

PERFORMATIVE WRITING

Performative writing is based on the principle that our words on the page communicate through form as much as they communicate through content. That is, that what we write and how we write it cannot be separated. Performative writing is as much intellectual as it is sensorial. It seeks to affectively capture in language some of the fleeting reality of performance broadly understood. It recognizes the limits of language in the search for objectivity and consciously renounces the idea that you can fully capture events, thoughts or feelings into words. Instead, understanding that language is limited, performative writing seeks to harness the poetic qualities of language in order to provoke emotional reactions in the reader. This kind of writing is performative not only because it refers to performance, but because the writing itself *does* something beyond merely reporting data. Like the performative function of language that we have reviewed in past chapters, performative writing has an effect on the world.

There are many authors in performance studies, some of which we have discussed throughout this book, whose writing diverges from and pushes the limits of what is commonly understood as scholarly writing. Performance studies scholars do not assume that there is only one right way of writing scholarship. Rather, they recognize that texts are powerful and that, when we read, we enter a text's universe with our senses, memories, emotions and expectations. Harnessing all of these sensorial dimensions of text can enrich scholarship without sacrificing its rigor. D. Soyini Madison structures her book *Acts of Activism* in three acts, following the structure of acts in a play, in order to explore different case studies about local human rights activists in Ghana. Fred Moten's *In the Break* plays with language and sentences in ways reminiscent of improvisation techniques in the jazz aesthetic of black musical traditions. Patrick Anderson includes excerpts in the autoethnography of his illness as if they were written from the point of view of the bacteria that infected him. In all these cases and many others, the experimentation with writing as an artistic form enriches the thought-provoking dimensions of the scholarship.

STAGING PERFORMANCE

Performance studies scholars are often also performance practitioners. They perform or direct performances, make films, write plays and scripts, make stage adaptations of a variety of dramatic and non-dramatic texts, curate art and performance events and create installations and a variety of digital media performances. They also often design performative activist interventions in civic life by combining multiple forms of art and protest, a subject that we cover in this book in the chapter dedicated to performance activism. Through these practices, performance studies scholars/practitioners demonstrate that material, embodied, non-textual modes of knowledge creation and diffusion are as important as textual ones. The staging of ethnographic research occupies a central place amongst these practices. In *Performed Ethnography & Communication*, D. Soyini Madison observes that creating performances from ethnographic research receives many different names, such as documentary theatre, non-fiction-storytelling, reality theatre, ethnographic performance and verbatim theatre. Madison prefers to encompass all these different ways of referring to the same phenomena as 'performed ethnography', a label that we will also use throughout this section.

Performed ethnography is the process through which we create theatrical performances starting from the materials and data collected during ethnographic fieldwork and stage them for different audiences. Despite its name, performed ethnography often involves the convergence between ethnographic and other research methods, such as archival and historiographic research. It also often brings together scholarly research, theatre and/or art practice and political activism.

The documentary performance *The (M)others,* written by performance scholar and practitioner Nikki Yeboah illustrates many of the potentials of performed ethnography. Yeboah created the script for *The (M)others* from interviews she conducted with women in the San Francisco Bay Area who have lost loved ones to police brutality. She then used verbatim excerpts from these interviews to weave a story in which four women come together to share their memories of their loved ones, as well as the events that led to their murders. By dramatizing the memory and experiences of these women, *The (M)others* allows audiences to access the events in their full complexity. We become deeply aware of the personal trauma and grief, as well as the joyful memories these mothers have of their children, years before they became victims of police violence. The performance also weaves the mothers' experiences with a broader social and political system – a system that is not built to help black and brown youth cope with poverty, unemployment, mental health issues or drug addiction, and yet keeps pouring resources into policing and restraining their bodies, often with tragic consequences.

Although *The (M)others* started as a live staged event created in 2019 that toured several theatrical spaces in and beyond the Bay Area, in the fall of 2020 and due to restrictions imposed on public gatherings during the COVID-19 pandemic, it became a multi-media performance event on Zoom. Upon reserving a ticket, each audience member was sent a link and instructions to connect online at the signalled date and time. The Zoom performance took the form of a conversation amongst the four actresses playing the mothers. During the performance, audiences were also encouraged to use the side group chat and communicate with the performers, either by answering specific questions or sharing their reactions at particular moments. The group chat also served as an online community in which audience members could express support for the mothers and the victims of police violence more broadly, or share resources about what to do in their local areas to prompt police reform. Practical information about a number of local organizations and instructions on how to call government representatives were also shared. The performance was followed by a Q&A that included Yeboah, the actresses and the director, as well as the real mothers on whose stories the performance was based. This format allowed audiences not only deeper insights into the creative process behind *The (M)others,* but also the possibility to engage with the real protagonists of these stories. During the Q&A, the creative team took a step back, holding space for the mothers to talk about their activism against police brutality. This tactic fell in line with the performance's general ethos to put artistic resources in service of the stories told, not to use the stories as the prime material from which a theatrical performance is created that remains isolated from everyday life.

This chapter has reviewed some of the primary methods used in performance studies to conduct research and present its results. Before embarking on a performance studies project, we might want to ask ourselves some of the following questions: Why is this relevant to people other than myself? What do I want to find out? What would be my data? How will I collect it? How will I make sense of it? What theories help me make sense of the phenomena I am studying? How will I report my findings? Who does this research benefit beyond myself?

FURTHER READING/RESEARCH

For a complete discussion on performance ethnography, consult:

Madison, D. Soyini. *Critical Ethnography: Method, Ethics, and Performance.* Thousand Oaks: SAGE Publications, 2020.

Further excellent examples of archival research and close readings not mentioned in this chapter can be found in:

Chambers-Letson, Joshua. *A Race So Different: Performance and Law in Asian America.* New York: New York University Press, 2013.
Gains, Malik. *Black Performance on the Outskirts of the Left: A History of the Impossible.* New York: New York University Press, 2017.
Hamera, Judith. *Parlor Ponds: The Cultural Work of the American Home Aquarium, 1850–1970.* Ann Arbor: University of Michigan Press, 2012.

In addition to the books mentioned throughout this chapter, watch:

Fires in the Mirror, George C. Wolfe, PBS (1993)
Making Sweet Tea, Marc Levin, PBS (2018)
Twilight: Los Angeles, John L. Jackson, Jr. (2000)

7

PERFORMANCE STUDIES

THE BIRTH OF PERFORMANCE STUDIES

Throughout the Western world, but especially in the United States, the 1960s and 1970s brought about developments that we have mentioned throughout this book, such as increased political activism from racial, sexual and gender minorities, and changes in the art world that led to the emergence of performance art. Societal transformations also reached higher education, transforming the humanities and social sciences in ways that made possible the consolidation of performance studies as a distinct academic field. This chapter provides an overview of how performance studies came to be. It is wise, however, to start that story with the caveat that many origin stories of the field cover its developments in the Anglo-speaking world, often unintentionally giving the impression that performance studies research only happens in the United States and the United Kingdom. The truth is that, depending on the methods used, the objects of study, the questions asked, and the geographical location, one can draw different histories of the field. And although this section covers the United States' trajectory of performance studies, the next section broadens the focus to performance studies research around the world. The second half of this chapter provides alternative views of the field – first, by pointing to the possible limitations of regarding performance as a socially liberatory force, and second, by speculating about where the field might be heading in the future.

A major transformation affecting higher education in the late 1960s was the questioning of the Eurocentrism inherent in the arts and humanities, their methods and their objects of study. Eurocentrism

DOI: 10.4324/9780429286377-8

meant that works by white men of Euro-American origins were considered the most important, and this implicitly rendered works by both minorities in the West and thinkers in non-Western geographical locations as less relevant. Eurocentrism was also responsible for why, in order to be considered an educated person, one had to be familiar with dramatic texts from Shakespeare to Samuel Beckett, and art works from Reubens to Picasso, but could completely ignore the artistic practices of other cultures. When considered at all, these artistic practices were regarded as inferior phenomena deserving only anthropological curiosity. The discipline of theatre studies was also immersed in this Eurocentric perspective. In universities, the study of theatre had been focused almost exclusively on dramatic literature, with the consequence that non-Western forms of performance could only be seen as primitive in comparison because they were not written in texts. With the aforementioned societal changes of the 1960s, it became clear to some that Eurocentrism had to be dismantled in higher education, and for those interested in the study of performance, this meant looking at actual embodied performance as much as dramatic texts.

Along with questioning the Eurocentric cultural canon in the arts and humanities, some scholars of theatre and rhetoric in the 1970s started to be interested in how their academic fields could be enriched by what anthropologists had to say about performance. In anthropology, performance was emerging at the time as a concept that explained the ways people within particular cultural traditions create meaning and values, how they symbolically communicate life experiences, and how they generate both social cohesion and social transformation. Scholars of performance turned to cultural anthropologists who were studying the points of contact between Western and non-Western cultural traditions. These anthropologists were suggesting that, instead of thinking about a hierarchy where Western cultural forms were superior, it was more accurate to think about differences across cultures without putting them in a hierarchy. In folklore studies and ethnomusicology, two subfields of anthropology, performance became an essential concept to theorize that folk art and musical traditions from across the world are not static objects but practices that constantly evolve. Unlike Western musical forms, many non-Western musical traditions did not need a score to be learned. Instead, they were passed down from one generation to the next through performance. So to understand these traditions, the study of music had to distance itself from scores and texts and embrace embodied events as the object of study.

In the United States, Northwestern University and New York University spearheaded the symbiosis of performance and anthropology. At Northwestern, inspired by the work of anthropologists such as Mary Douglas (1921–2007) and Clifford Geertz (1926–2006), Dwight Conquergood saw performance as an essential element that influences the ever-changing process of culture. Conquergood was chairing Northwestern's department of Oral Interpretation, a subfield of rhetoric and communication studies dedicated to the study and presentation of literature through techniques of staged performance. Closer to public speaking than acting, oral interpretation consisted of a series of techniques meant to illuminate the elements and meaning of literary texts through oral presentation. As performance studies scholar and former Conquergood student Shannon Jackson has astutely noted, the dilemmas that anthropologists were facing in the 1980s when trying to explain foreign cultures resonated with the dilemmas of oral interpretation scholars, namely representing the plurality of voices, points of view, intentions and narrative shifts in a text through performance. In other words, both fields were concerned with the ways in which we access and understand the worlds of people whose experiences we have never had, whether those people were characters in literature or people from cultures very different from our own. Understanding these similarities, Conquergood believed that performance's attention to detail and its vocabulary to describe embodied everyday encounters could enrich ethnography.

While Conquergood arrived at performance studies through oral interpretation, at New York University, scholar and avant-garde theatre director Richard Schechner arrived at performance studies through an interest in the universal structure of drama. Turning to anthropologist Victor Turner's ideas on 'social dramas', Schechner argued that the same structure that occurs in social conflicts can be found in all theatre. Turner had determined that in many societies around the world social transformation happened in a four-step process. First, the existing social tensions cause a breach. Then, the breach opens up a period of crisis. To address the crisis, some redressive action has to take place. Lastly, after the redressive action, there is a phase of social reintegration that either brings groups back together in harmony or fully separates them forever. Following this model, Schechner argued that all social conflicts, such as wars, political crises, criminal trials or everyday disputes, are not that different in structure from Shakespearean dramas or Greek ancient theatre. While NYU's borrowing from anthropology expanded the canon of traditional theatre studies by including performance from non-Western cultures, Northwestern's anthropological methods served to reflect on the inherent power dynamics of collecting and performing other people's stories. These early cross-overs between anthropology, rhetoric and theatre, alongside the contributions of sociologists like Erving Goffman and linguists like J. L. Austin that have been discussed in previous chapters, account for why in the United States performance studies scholarship has always been at least as close to the social sciences as to theatre and performance art.

In the early 1980s, performance studies started to coalesce into a defined academic discipline when Schechner's Drama Department at NYU and Conquergood's Department of Oral Interpretation at Northwestern officially changed their names to Performance Studies. After that initial shift, departments of Performance Studies emerged at other institutions, and many existing departments of theatre and communications changed their names and curricula to accommodate performance studies degrees and scholarship. Former students from NYU and Northwestern got academic jobs all over the country, creating a national performance studies network that was hosted in different departments. In the 1990s, international conferences specialized in performance studies were formed, and performance studies focus groups were established in major theatre and communication conferences in the United States. This structure helped the field grow from the 1990s onward, as performance studies scholars from across the world came together and exchanged ideas and practices in these and other meetings. In addition, starting in the late 1990s, international scholars formed in the United States, many at Northwestern and NYU, returned to their home countries, introduced performance studies departments, programs and curricula, and started putting into dialogue their academic training with local performance practices. That being said, a critique that is often brought up within the field is that histories of the development of performance studies that emphasize its US-American origin contribute to a hierarchy in which performance studies research from other locations occupies a secondary place. The following section will contextualize US–American performance studies vis-à-vis performance research around the world.

PERFORMANCE STUDIES AROUND THE WORLD

Although academic departments under the specific rubric of performance studies are found mostly in the English-speaking world, specifically in the United States, United Kingdom, Canada and Australia, performance studies scholarship is produced globally by scholars in departments and disciplines under other names, such as communication, theatre, dance, music, media, anthropology, sociology and art history, among others. The social science orientation of performance studies that is widespread in the United States is, however, less characteristic of how performance studies developed in many other places around the world. This section maps out some of those differences within the field of performance studies across geographical locations.

In the United Kingdom, performance studies usually refers to the study of experimental theatre and performance, audience reception practices around the performing arts, and the relationship between performance practice and theory that happens in theatre and art spaces. When the word 'interdisciplinarity' is deployed in this context, it tends to refer to the mixing of disciplines under the umbrella of the performing arts, such as theatre, dance, music and performance art. Besides specific organisms, like the Centre for Performance Research, founded in 1988 and located in Aberystwyth, UK-based performance studies scholars and scholarship have tended to be hosted in theatre and drama departments of a multitude of universities. Rather than offering specific programs in performance studies, performance theory and methods are integrated across the curricula of theatre and drama at places such as Aberystwyth University, University of Limerick, University of Bristol, University of Leeds, and Roehampton, Queen Mary College and King's College in London.

Due to this institutional structure, most performance studies scholarship in the United Kingdom stems from a narrower definition of performance as staged artistic practices than its United States counterpart. In fact, some of the most passionate resistance against US-based scholars' alleged tendency to 'calling everything performance' has come from theatre academics based in the UK. The fervour of many of these critiques seems warranted if one understands them as a response to some US-based performance studies scholars' earlier critique of theatre studies. For example, at the 1992 Association for Theatre in Higher Education (ATHE) conference, Richard Schechner declared that theatre studies was dead and out of touch with the contemporary global world by only studying European drama. This oversimplification, which was arguably not fair to theatre studies scholars across the board, unnecessarily ruffled the feathers of many of them. UK theatre and performance scholar Stephen Bottoms wrote a rigorous critique of Schechner's dismissal of dramatic literature, while Alan Read denounced what he saw as performance studies broadening its scope to include a lot of things as performance yet failing to simultaneously examine the methodological efficacy of this. Read argued that, while performance studies was establishing itself as a distinct field, theatre studies had already been employing a performance studies methodology by addressing artistic experimentation and its relationship with social and political life. These debates show us that, paradoxically, for all of the overlaps of theatre studies and performance studies in their objects of study and their methods, some of the most vicious critiques of either of these fields have come from the other.

Since the 1990s, performance studies research and performance studies departments have developed outside of the Anglo-American context. In Asia, performance studies researchers initially coalesced around institutions such as the Shanghai Theatre Academy and the University of Singapore. Additionally, in China and Japan, a particular form of performance studies emerged that focused on the study of performance in everyday life and its application to maximize productivity and personal empowerment in people's social roles. Distancing itself from the Anglo-American brand of performance studies as cultural critique, this brand of performance studies sought to provide useful behavioural training to businessmen, politicians, government officials and lawyers who were seeking to thrive in the global economy.

In Australia, performance studies curricula and researchers found a home at major universities, such as the University of Melbourne and the University of Sidney. Akin to the United Kingdom, Australian performance studies has mainly consisted of the scholarly study of staged performance practices and rehearsal processes. Due to proximity to Asia, performance studies in Australia has also tended towards a regional focus including the study of performance practices from local Asian contexts, such as *wayang kulit*, an Indonesian shadow puppetry genre.

A critique that has accompanied the development of performance studies since the late 1990s is that, despite its intended global focus, the majority of performance studies researchers are located within Anglo-speaking institutions and countries. This fuelled many internal debates in the field, as some people felt that performance studies was imperialist and engaging in some of the very colonizing structures that it critiques. For its critics, further evidence of this colonizing project was the fact that most performance studies publishing happened in English at academic presses located in the United States and the United Kingdom. And while this scholarship travelled to other locations frequently, performance scholarship written in languages other than English less frequently travelled to performance studies scholars in United States and the United Kingdom. In this respect, performance studies is not different from any other contemporary academic discipline that uses English as the lingua franca of the global world. However, for a field that thinks of itself as transgressive, anti-colonial and committed to uplifting the voices of those in the margins of society, performance studies constantly struggles with the power hierarchies inherent in its dependence on English for international circulation. As we enter the third decade of the twenty-first century, and even though the locations where performance studies research happens have kept expanding in the last few decades, the field still grapples with the imperialist question. Many researchers and practitioners who describe their work as performance studies are located in places as diverse as Morocco, Indonesia, Croatia, Slovenia, South Africa, Israel, Greece, Singapore or Hong Kong, to name a few. While many of them have been academically trained in the United States or the United Kingdom, it would be incorrect to assume that this only underscores the Anglo-American dominance within the field. In fact, in these locations, many US- and UK-trained performance researchers productively blend their training with local performance traditions, histories and critical perspectives, creating work that is uniquely positioned to critique the power hierarchies in the field.

Another common critique that has fuelled internal debates is that the very name 'performance studies' is tied to the Anglo-American context dominating the field. This has prompted some scholars to suggest that 'performance research' is a better name for it. However, this renaming is still unlikely to solve the larger power imbalance between the English-speaking world and the rest. This imbalance is also determined by the fact that the word 'performance' does not have exact translations in other languages. In both Spanish and German, for example, the word 'performance' does exist as an English neologism, but it is used to refer only to performance art. Beyond performance art, other objects of study of English-speaking performance studies, such as the performative aspects of everyday life, the performativity of gender, or the representation of race and difference, are studied in the Spanish and German contexts under other names and departments. This makes it harder for researchers under different institutional affiliations across the world to recognize each other as part of the same field. Moreover, performance studies research happens around the world in the practice of performance groups, multimedia artists, theatre makers, dancers, burlesque and drag performers, circus workers and art activists who are often not affiliated with academic institutions and might describe their work in ways that do not always overlap with those of performance studies academics.

Performance studies in the global context is also often divided by regional affiliations. Within those regions, one finds specific networks and transnational organisms, such as The Hemispheric Institute of Performance and Politics (Hemi) or the Asian Performance Studies Research Group. Hemi was founded at NYU in 1998, and it is an interdisciplinary network of institutions and people throughout the Americas whose work is located at the intersection of scholarship, artistic practice and politics. Working in three languages, Spanish, Portuguese and English, Hemi has organized courses, workshops, conferences and festivals in its two-decades of existence, while also keeping an archive and digital video library with hundreds of hours of recorded performances. The Asian Performance Studies Research Group emerged in 2003 as a gathering of performance studies academics and practitioners around an annual meeting of PSi, the Performance Studies international annual conference. The Asian Performance Studies Research Group ushered an important tendency toward the formation of regional clusters that has marked the 2010s. Regional clusters often coalesce in regional conferences and form networks in which performance studies researchers from different locations around the world interact with each other without the need to interact with the field's Anglo-American centre. The tendency towards regionalization culminated in the totally decentralized organization of the 2015 PSi conference. Instead of the traditional annual encounter in one location, the conference consisted of activities taking place across Africa, Asia, Australia, Europe, the Americas and the Pacific region throughout the entirety of 2015 under the title 'Fluid States'.

As we enter the 2020s, these global developments of performance studies research respond to an interesting paradox. On the one hand, the multitude of performance studies clusters across the globe have been a result of the global expansion of United States culture and economy. One particularly controversial aspect of this expansion has entailed the restructuring of universities around the world to function more like American universities, which in turn function more and more like for-profit corporations in which interdisciplinarity and the crosspollination of knowledge production and creativity respond to the demands of flexible economies and ever-changing markets. On the other hand, it seems desirable for the health of the field of performance studies to continue multiplying locally to a point in which the Anglo-American origin of the discipline is no longer its centre. Hopefully, the local and regional proliferation of performance studies research in many different areas of the world will continue in the future, until the Anglo-American origins of performance studies will be just one among many other histories that are told of the field. Two books that explore different strands and regional histories of performance studies are *Contesting Performance: Global Sites of Research*, edited by Jon McKenzie, Heike Roms and C. J.W.-L Wee, and *The Rise of Performance Studies*, edited by James M. Harding and Cindy Rosenthal.

PERFORMANCE AND THE STATUS QUO

Despite the wide variety of forms that performance studies takes around the world, looking at the past five decades, what seems certain is that the field as a whole has tended to highlight the edgy, transgressive and politically radical potential of performance. The majority of performance studies scholarship to date has explored the ability of performance broadly understood to intervene in oppressive social conditions and allow communities to envision and rehearse projects of freedom, equality and justice. However, if, in theory, an endless array of individual and social actions can be studied *as* performance, then actions that are the opposite of liberatory are also performances. If everyday life events can be studied *as* performance, are the Black Lives Matter protests more of a performance than the interventions of police officers shooting rubber bullets and tear gas at them? Doesn't gender performativity mean that our individual behaviours can reinforce oppressive gender expectations as much as they can unsettle them? Can't the parody of the colonial gaze in Coco Fusco and Gómez Peña's 'Couple in the Cage' fall flat with the spectators who actually believed them to be savages, actually reinforcing these people's previous stereotypes about indigenous populations? Why, then, does the field of performance studies largely insist on emphasizing the transgressive potential of performance, but almost never its ability to reinforce the status quo? This is a complex question that we will explore in this section.

Despite remaining marginal in performance studies scholarship, some theoretical contributions have offered grounds to understand performance as a force that also upholds the status quo. Contributions studying the conservative potential of performance have tended to remain marginal in the field, though not because of an oversight of performance studies scholars. Instead, they remain marginal because, despite the field's purported positioning against norms, regarding performance as transgressive might be precisely its most important norm. This does not mean that performance studies scholars do not recognize that performance can make social norms as much as it can break them, but that, while recognizing that possibility, they still overwhelmingly emphasize the ability of performance to change the world for the better.

If we were to adopt a sceptical view of the role of performance in bringing about social justice, we would turn to the work of philosophers such as Jean-Francois Lyotard (1924–1998) and Herbert Marcuse (1898–1979), and performance studies scholars such as Jon McKenzie, among others. These are not the only intellectual contributions to studying the role of performance in maintaining power, but they are some of the most significant.

In his 1955 book *Eros and Civilization,* German philosopher Herbert Marcuse argued that a 'performance principle' governs reality in Western civilization. Under capitalism, this performance principle makes society work according to the maximization of production and profit. This means that when workers perform their labour, they do not work only to cover their own economic needs but also to produce wealth for a capitalist class. To translate this to our contemporary moment, we can think, for instance, how a worker making burgers at McDonalds or assembling electronics for Apple, not only works to pay their rent, buy clothes and afford food, but also for the purpose of accumulating wealth for the corporation that employs them. This is wealth that the worker will never enjoy, but which benefits those who are higher up, such as executives and shareholders. Though highly unfair for working classes, this arrangement is maintained, according to Marcuse, because workers' desire for change is repressed by the 'performance principle' that prompts them to maintain their roles. In other words, the performance principle is the tendency to keep performing one's social role. At large scale, this performance principle assures the smooth functioning of the economic system as people tend to repress those impulses of human nature that conflict with the function they perform in society. At the individual level, the performance principle is internalized as the natural behaviour needed to fulfil one's social role to the point that it is not consciously felt as repression. For Marcuse, the performance principle is the reason why workers do not revolt en masse to change their labour conditions. Although Marcuse's performance principle predates Judith Butler's writings by a few decades, we can also think of the performance principle and the performativity of gender in similar ways. Just like we enter a matrix of expected gender behaviours when we are born and we continue to internalize them until they feel natural, we also enter an economic social arrangement and we internalize the behaviours and norms that shape our participation in it, making it seem natural. According to this principle, it seems natural to sell one's labour to corporations that profit from it and barely pay living wages, it seems natural to work long hours, or that food, shelter or life-saving drugs are accessible on a for-profit market rather than universally guaranteed to all people. We can see how this view of performance, far from transgressive, in fact explains how people repeat and naturalize behaviours that subject them.

After Marcuse, French philosopher Jean-Francois Lyotard published his book *The Postmodern Condition* in 1979. In the book, Lyotard argued that since the mid-twentieth century, scientific and technological research in Western capitalist societies functions according to a principle of performativity. According to this principle, knowledge ceases to be an end in itself. Instead, what drives technological innovation is a push for increased efficiency tied to capital and generating wealth. Becoming synonymous with efficiency, performativity is the best possible input/output equation in any scientific and technological endeavour. Prior ideals inherited from the Enlightenment, which saw the production and dissemination of knowledge as a benefit in the emancipation of humanity, disappear in favour of a view of knowledge that seeks to augment power. Lyotard also thinks performativity works as a self-fulfilling circular criterion. This means that technological advancements are valued primarily in terms of performing well and, in turn, performing well becomes the ultimate truth according to which all things are measured. Much like Marcuse's performance principle, Lyotard's performativity is not liberatory but is complicit in the maintenance of oppressive forms of power brought about by modern capitalism.

Unlike many of their contemporary philosophers and literary theorists, Marcuse and Lyotard are not often cited in the field of performance studies, perhaps because it is presumably hard to reconcile their grim views on performance and performativity with the more liberatory focus of performance studies. One exception to this oversight is performance studies scholar Jon McKenzie. In his book *Perform or Else,* McKenzie poses the question of how it is that theories that present a normative view of performance remain marginal in the field. The reason, McKenzie thinks, is not that performance studies scholars do not know these theories or do not believe them, but that performance studies as a field functions according to its own norms, and the main norm is underscoring the transgressive potential in performance.

McKenzie also notes that in the United States after World War II, performance has proliferated all over society, albeit deployed to mean very different things. For example, in the organizational world of corporations, non-profits, government agencies and other institutions, performance is a metric to measure the efficiency of human labour, exemplified by so-called 'performance reviews' that guide economic decisions. This has given rise to a paradigm of *organizational performance* that has been developing for at least as long as performance studies, yet that has no relationship whatsoever with the latter. In the applied sciences, performance is a vaguely defined but popular concept that refers to the effective functioning of something, from computer systems, weapons and chemical compounds to cars and home appliances. This is a paradigm of *technological performance* and, as with organizational performance, it has had no relationship with performance studies. Yet, despite the apparent separation of these different spheres of performance, McKenzie suggests that they all have a common cause. They all come from a shift in mid-twentieth-century American society, which started to transition to an understanding of power as defined by performance. Due to the global dominance of the United States, McKenzie believes that this social model is now the worldwide paradigm through which society functions. Whereas power previously resided in the social institutions that regulated individual behaviours, such as courts of justice, governments, the police or schools, for McKenzie, twenty-first-century power resides in the compulsion to perform. Technology, organizations and individuals must all perform according to norms of efficiency and efficacy in the economic system.

The historical coincidences McKenzie finds between the rise of organizational performance, technological performance and performance studies elicits interesting questions: Is it a coincidence that the same society that compels individuals to perform according to rules of high efficiency also gave birth to an academic field that argues that all human behaviour can be regarded as performance? What does it mean that these processes emerged at the same time as a global expansion of capitalism that encourages the elimination of barriers between life and work? In other words, if to perform is do something according to criteria that maximizes efficiency, and if all our behaviours are potentially performance, is there any room left for behaviours that are inefficient, idle, non-productive and, in general, not susceptible to becoming work? Can we even stop performing in a society that has mastered surveillance technologies to the point that our everyday activities leave a digital trace, always making us susceptible of being watched and having an audience? Is performing just another word for having one's behaviour always on display and consequently fully visible to corporations and government agencies?

These are questions that do not have simple answers and their scope lays beyond the purpose of this book and the capabilities of its author. It might even seem strange to the reader that a book full of examples in which humans perform to transform the world into a better place might turn to a sombre tone towards the end by pointing that contemporary capitalism invites us to perform compulsively. And yet, it is necessary to raise the possibility that, far from being simply liberatory, performance is very often an essential instrument in maintaining the status quo with all its injustices. If power hierarchies are maintained through performance, we have to wonder whether an intellectual project that invites us to see the whole world as performance might be more complicit than transgressive. We also have to wonder whether performing – sharing a meal, protesting on the street, sharing activist content on social media, dancing during a carnival, moving our bodies against gender expectations, telling stories and many other things – is often how, in a performative society, the poor and the oppressed can have temporary experiences of pleasure so that they feel less inclined to revolt. The purpose of admitting the normative power of performance is not to debunk the field of performance studies. Rather, it is to push the field's critical agenda even further. For, if contemporary capitalism cannot function without performance or, in other words, if contemporary capitalism is performative, how might taking that seriously reorient the future work of performance studies scholars and practitioners who care about justice, equality and freedom?

SPECULATIVE FUTURES OF PERFORMANCE STUDIES

After a brief overview of the field and its history, this section offers a tentative exploration of where performance studies might go in the future.

First, as previously suggested, a serious consideration of how performance might reify some of the most conservative, even oppressive, elements of contemporary society remains largely untapped as a subject of research. After all, can we separate that millions of people in the United States believed Donald Trump could be a capable president from the fact that he played the part of a capable businessman for years on reality television? Does performing even stop in the contemporary gig economy for an ever-increasing number of people who must survive by selling themselves constantly as the ultimate hot commodity? Aren't the small, unnoticed everyday performances that become habits through repetition what keeps us attached to social roles and structures that often do not benefit us? Our behaviours as consumers of goods whose production hurts our planet and which subjects workers to strenuous labour conditions, our compliance with job expectations that make us unhappy and our disciplined movements through public spaces that are engineered for the accumulation of capital are all examples of everyday performances that maintain the status quo. Performance therefore can be an instrument of social change and freedom as much as an instrument of oppression. This suggests the field of performance studies could expand in new directions if at least as much attention was given to the normative works of performance as to the ways in which performance is used for sustaining and celebrating life in the face of oppression.

Second, the so-called 'posthuman turn' that the arts and humanities have experienced in the first couple of decades of the twentieth century is likely to usher even more radical re-examinations of what is meant by terms such as 'embodiment' and even the 'body'. The posthuman turn comes from the consolidation of interdisciplinary fields, such as animal studies, environmental humanities, eco-criticism, new materialism and indigenous studies, which taken together have served to critically re-examine the definition of 'human' on which most Western intellectual inquiry has been based until now. Prior to the so-called posthuman turn, the Western idea of the human developed alongside colonialism and became dominant after the Enlightenment and the eighteenth-century liberal revolutions, such as the American Revolution and the French Revolution. Though supposedly a universal conception of the human, in practice, Enlightenment thinkers narrowly defined the human as an autonomous and rational being completely separated from nature. Because of his capability to exercise free will and communicate through language, the human was deemed superior to all other species inhabiting the planet, and consequently, with the right to exploit them to his benefit.

To be sure, the intersection of performance studies with feminist and queer theory, on the one hand, and critical theory in ethnicity and race, on the other, helped the field consider the particularities of embodied experience since at least the 1980s. And yet, performance studies still has much to gain from further questioning the body as a discrete, autonomous entity. With the posthuman turn, animal studies has shown us that we simply cannot afford to consider the human as an exceptional species if we want to prevent environmental catastrophes. Indigenous studies has advocated for sustainable forms of relating to the environment that colonized and indigenous communities practiced before, after, and despite the arrival of white Europeans. New materialism has abolished the distinction between animate and inanimate matter, suggesting that we are biologically entangled with every material that exists on the planet, from minerals and water to the plastics that we produce and that find their ways back into our bodies via our food chains. Disability studies has prompted us to consider that the body is greatly shaped by the environment in which it moves, that disability is a spectrum, and that, at different points in the process of a human life, all bodies might experience some form of disability. In light of these theoretical perspectives, what is a body? Where do my body, my bodily autonomy, and my embodied performances start and end? How might the performances of a human body reverberate to other forms of matter, both biological and non-biological?

Moreover, if we admit that the human should not be taken as the ultimate measure with which knowledge is created and research is conducted, how does this change the ways in which we have defined performance? Our reader might remember that the introduction to this book started by asserting that *homo sapiens* is, in fact, *homo performans*, but is performance still a useful instrument to study social life if we zoom out to include not only humans but also other species, objects, inanimate matter and the interactions amongst all of them in our inquiry? After all, it seems that performance necessitates some sort of agency, of undertaking an action and communicating it to others, no matter how unconscious, automatic or unintentional that behaviour might be. Can objects, animals and matter perform? If so, what is performance, then? Has performance as an instrument to analyse the world been anthropocentric, that is, centred exclusively on *homo sapiens*? How might a human-centred definition of performance shift towards an interspecies and eco-conscious paradigm? As the limits of what we understand by performance keep expanding, do they reach a point in which they stop being useful to understand the world?

Third, despite remarkable attempts to theorize embodied live performance in its relationship with technology and media, the fact remains that a lot of performance studies research, and most of all, performance studies' teaching seems to need face-to-face, physical encounters. Societal changes such as those prompted by the global COVID-19 pandemic and its restrictions to live interactions likely indicate that there still remains a lot of work to be done to explore the possibilities of performance, and what performance might even mean, when human bodies are not co-performing in the same space at the same time. Defining performance for these emerging societal changes would go beyond the traditional idea that technological mediation is part of embodied encounters. What happens when the live is actually not possible at all, and all that is available is the online, remote and technologically mediated? Has performance studies been so far too reliant on the transformative dimension of embodied live encounters? Or, quite the opposite, is it wise to give up on the idea that true transformative performances must include some sort of live interaction?

Finally, in light of all the previous points, we might speculate that just as performance studies scholarship and research will have to further grapple with the normative power of performance and the nature of bodies as entanglements of matter, rather than discrete entities, so will performance activism and performance practice more broadly.

WHY PERFORMANCE STUDIES, THEN?

If, as a reader, you have reached this point in the book, you might wonder if/why pursuing a performance studies career is a good choice for you. If you are an activist or a performance practitioner of any kind, whether in performance art, theatre, dance, stand-up, circus, drag, burlesque, etc., you are probably already aware that there are many paths to build a career in the performance practice of your choosing, and you might not need to formally pursue a performance studies degree to reach your professional, artistic or activist goals. In fact, do not expect that all performance studies departments and/or programs will be prepared, able or interested in accommodating your specific performance practice and helping you develop it. Some of them might, and in order to decide which ones do, you will need to do a little digging on your own by researching university websites and getting in touch with specific academic departments to ask questions.

If you are interested in pursuing a performance studies degree, there are many reasons to do so. At its best, performance studies provides a framework to analyse and understand artistic practice and its relationships to society as well as the performative aspects of identity and how they are influenced by power and history. It also allows us to analyse and understand how people effectively mobilize in collective political action that can be beautiful and transformative. More broadly, performance studies gives us a framework to understand the role of the body in the creation of meaning and culture. More than anything, pursuing a performance studies degree will provide a solid ground for you to develop your critical and creative thinking, will sharpen your perception to understand the world around you and will spark your imagination to intervene on it. These are things that you will find useful for everything else you might want to do in life.

If you are looking to pursue a graduate degree in performance studies, and eventually a career as a performance studies scholar/practitioner, the previous paragraph also applies to you, but a few extra caveats are necessary. First, be aware that the commodification of knowledge and the management of universities according to corporate models are decisive factors in your future career. Graduate students, postdocs and non-tenured instructors are profitable for universities because they do a lot of teaching for little money, which is why universities produce many more doctors than the ones that can realistically remain in academia long term. This means that a tenured or stable career in higher education may not exist for you after your graduate degree. Second, in the corporate university, interdisciplinarity is often another name for flexible labour, as junior scholars have to be able to respond to multiple requirements to find jobs in the midst of ever-changing, ever-shrinking labour opportunities and conditions. Third, and more importantly, even though, in theory, everything can be studied *as* performance, in reality not everything that is studied *as* performance is likely to get you a job *in* performance studies, or even academia at large. Despite the language of subversion that has come to define the discipline, performance studies in fact does have more or less clear disciplinary boundaries. As a junior scholar you will have to navigate the tension between a training that has taught you the whole world is performance and a much more limited range of available jobs in specific departments and fields, with particular research objects and methodologies.

All of these circumstances may make one working in performance studies feel sometimes jaded, because as we are critically trained to expose structures of power, we also have to participate in an economic model based on scarcity and which commodifies knowledge and scholarship. Despite the grim landscape that I just painted for you, I would advise you not to despair. Should you choose to, pursue your performance studies degree with an open mind for what your career might look like in the end. Think about what you would like to do in the world. Include in that thinking practical ways to make a living, but also what impact you want to have on others, what social issues are important to you, what creative projects nurture your imagination and what makes you feel fulfilled, or in other words, as my advisor, D. Soyini Madison, says, think about 'the work that your soul needs'. With that in mind, keep an eye out for the venues where you can do those things beyond higher education or performance studies scholarship, whether in your performance practice, curatorial roles, arts administration, cultural non-profits and foundations, government jobs, arts education, public scholarship or activist grassroots projects in your local community. The point is, a performance studies graduate degree can prepare you for many more things than you initially think, and you are not supposed to have all the answers before the journey starts.

GLOSSARY

Activism   An individual's action or collective mobilization to bring about social change.

Aesthetics   The form or style of something. Also, the scholarly study of how things look and appear.

Archive   The preservation of performance. Also, the preservation of records and historical materials, such as legal documents, personal diaries, letters, clothing, photographs, video, etc.

Authenticity   A series of value judgements that evaluate performances in relationship to the identity of the people who produce them.

Avant-garde   Art works and artists that are experimental and innovative for the standard of their time.

Body   A live physical structure in relationship with other such structures.

Body-modification   A deliberate alteration of one's anatomy or appearance for aesthetic purposes, ritual or religious beliefs. Common contemporary forms of body-modification include piercing, tattooing, scarification and implants.

Capitalism   An economic system based on the continuous extraction of wealth from people's labour in order to benefit a social elite.

Commodification   The process of turning something into a commodity and putting it up for sale.

Critical Theory   A set of evidence-based ideas applied to the study of society and culture in order to contribute to human emancipation and liberation.

Culture   An ongoing process through which a group of people perform common values, worldviews, histories and ways of being in the world.

Difference   That which orders social groups into categories according to identity markers.

Discourse   A system of thought, knowledge and communication that shapes human perception of particular topics.

Embodiment   The process of taking bodily form.

Ephemerality   A quality belonging to things that only last for a very short time and then disappear.

Ethnography   A relationship between someone conducting research and the particular culture, society or community that they study.

Eurocentrism   A biased worldview that favours people, cultures and political systems of European and, by extension, Western origins.

Event   Something that happens and which has a clear beginning and end, often a performance.

Feminism   A movement that advocates for women's rights on the basis that all people are equal.

Flash mob   A sudden gathering of a group of people to perform together in a public space, generally organized through social media.

Gender   An enactment of social conventions that becomes internalized by the individual.

Gender Studies   An interdisciplinary field that studies the social construction of gender, often also paying attention to how gender intersects with other categories such as race, ethnicity or class.

Heteronormative   A system, group or person that promotes heterosexuality as the normal or most desirable sexual orientation.

Historiography   The process of writing history and conducting historical research.

Identity   A process composed of an individual's performances of self, their appearance and the qualities, traits and histories attributed to them.

Interdisciplinary   Academic work that combines two or more traditional disciplines or fields of study.

Iteration   The repetition of an utterance or an act.

Kinetic   Related to the movement of a body.

Liberatory   Something that has the potential to bring about liberation or freedom.

Liveness   The quality of a performance that happens live, and in which all participants are in the same space and time.

Mediation/Mediatization   The circulation of performance through various forms of media.

Method   A process for solving a research problem through clear and identifiable steps, such as the gathering of data, its analysis and the pronouncement of specific conclusions.

Mimesis   Imitation or similarity.

Minoritarian   A person or group whose identity renders them a minority in society, as well as the culture, aesthetic tastes and artforms produced by these groups.

Normative/Normativity   That which upholds dominant norms and standards of behaviour in society.

Patriarchy   A social system in which men hold more power than any other group, and in which masculinity and all things masculine are valued more than any other genders.

Performative   Related to performativity. Or, in some performance studies scholarship, those elements of culture that resist various forms of oppression.

Performativity   Embodied behaviour resulting from processes of socialization and that is naturalized by repetition.

Power   A form of direct control or indirect influence over subjects' behaviour.

Practice   An embodied repetition of behaviour with the goal to improve or master it.

Presence   The ability to be modified by another.

Psychoanalysis   A set of psychological theories about the unconscious mind used in the study of literature, art and performance and which inform understandings of identity, gender, sexuality or race.

Queer   A non-normative sexual and/or gender identity.

Queer Studies   An interdisciplinary field that not only studies queer communities and experiences, but also more broadly the social construction of sexuality and gender.

Radical That which belongs to collective struggles against oppression and works towards social change.

Re-enactment The acting out of past historical events as a means to keep them alive.

Representation Depiction or portrayal of something or someone.

Reproduction The process of capturing, copying and circulating performance through technological means.

Ritual Collective performances that follow a set of established rules and mark a transition or special moment in a person's or a community's life.

Semiotics The study of signs and symbols.

Sensorial In performance, that which is related to the senses and is embodied and exceeding language.

Sociality A form of being together.

Speech Act An utterance that not only expresses something but constitutes a form of action with consequences.

Subjectivity The process through which a person comes to understand themselves in relation to others.

Symbol Something that stands in for something else.

Transgressive Willing to violate social and artistic boundaries, especially those based on conservative moral sensibilities.

Visibility One's ability to appear and be seen in public or society at large.

Visuality The socially shaped way in which we interpret and give meaning to what we observe through our eyes.

Western A colonial and capitalist perspective of the world.

BIBLIOGRAPHY

Alexander, Bryant Keith. *Performing Black Masculinity*. Lanham: AltaMira Press, 2006.

Alexander Craft, Renée. *When the Devil Knocks: The Congo Tradition and the Politics of Blackness in Twentieth-Century Panama*. Columbus: Ohio State University Press, 2015.

Anderson, Patrick. *Autobiography of a Disease*. New York: Routledge, 2017.

Auslander, Philip. *Liveness: Performance in a Mediatized Culture*. London; New York: Routledge, 1999.

Austin, J. L. *How to do Things with Words*. Cambridge: Harvard University Press, 1962.

Bauman, Richard. *Verbal Art as Performance*. Long Grove: Waveland Press, 1984.

Bell, Elisabeth. *Theories of Performance*. Thousand Oaks: SAGE Publications, 2008.

Bial, Henry, and Sara Brady. *The Performance Studies Reader*. 3rd edn. Abingdon; New York: Routledge, 2016.

Bottoms, Stephen. 'In Defense of the String Quartet: An Open Letter to Richard Schechner', in J. Harding and C. Rosenthal, eds, *The Rise of Performance Studies*. Basingstoke: Palgrave Macmillan, 2011: 23–38.

Brayshaw, Teresa, Anna Fenemore and Noel Witts. *The Twenty-First Century Performance Reader*. New York; Abingdon: Routledge, 2019.

Brooks, Daphne. *Bodies in Dissent: Spectacular Performances of Race and Freedom, 1850–1910*. Durham: Duke University Press, 2006.

Butler, Judith. *Bodies that Matter: On the Discursive Limits of Sex*. New York: Routledge, 2011.

Carlson, Marvin. 'Performance Studies and the Enhancement of Theatre Studies', in J. Harding and C. Rosenthal, eds, *The Rise of Performance Studies: Rethinking Richard Schechner's Broad Spectrum*. London: Palgrave Macmillan, 2011: 13–22.

Carlson, Marvin. *Performance: A Critical Introduction*. 3rd edn. New York: Routledge, 2017.

Cervera, Felipe. 'Planetary Performance Studies'. *Global Performance Studies* 1, no. 1 (2017).

Chaudhuri, Una. *The Stage Lives of Animals: Zooësis and Performance*. Abingdon; New York: Routledge, 2017.

Chung, Kelly I. 'The Defiant Still Worker: Ramiro Gomez and the Expressionism of Abstract Labor', *Women & Performance* 29, no. 1 (2019): 62–76.

Chung, Kelly I. 'Sleepwalking Slowly: Kat Eng and the Feminist Art of Living Labor in Common Time'. *ASAP Journal* 4, no. 3 (2019): 601–618.

Cohen-Cruz, Jan. *Radical Street Performance: An International Anthology*. London; New York: Routledge, 1998.

Collins, Lisa. *The Art of History: African American Women Artists Engage the Past*. New Brunswick: Rutgers University Press, 2002.

Concannon, Kevin. 'Yoko Ono's "Cut Piece": From Text to Performance and Back Again'. *PAJ* 30, no. 3 (2008): 81–93.

Conquergood, Dwight. *Cultural Struggles: Performance, Ethnography, Praxis*. Ed. E. Patrick Johnson. Ann Arbor: University of Michigan Press, 2013.

Davis, Tracy C. *The Cambridge Companion to Performance Studies*. Cambridge: Cambridge University Press, 2009.

Davis, Tracy C., and Peter W. Marx. *The Routledge Companion to Theatre and Performance Historiography*. New York: Routledge, 2020.

DeFrantz, Thomas F., and Anita Gonzalez. *Black Performance Theory*. Durham: Duke University Press, 2014.

De Laurentis, Teresa. 'On the Subject of Fantasy', in L. Pietropaulo and A. Testaferri, eds, *Feminisms in the Cinema*. Bloomington: Indiana University Press, 1995: 63–65.

Derrida, Jacques. 'Signature Event Context', in *Limited Inc*. Translated by Samuel Webber. Evanston: Northwestern University Press, 1988: 1–23.

Diamond, Elin. *Unmaking Mimesis: Essays on Feminism and Theatre*. New York: Routledge, 1993.

Diamond, Elin. 'Introduction', in E. Diamond, ed., *Performance and Cultural Politics*. New York: Routledge, 1996: 1–12.

Dolan, Jill. *Geographies of Learning: Theories and Practice, Activism and Performance*. Middletown: Wesleyan University Press, 2001.

Dolan, Jill. *Utopia in Performance: Finding Hope at the Theatre*. Ann Arbor: University of Michigan Press, 2010.

Doyle, Jennifer. *Hold It Against Me: Difficulty and Emotion in Contemporary Art*. Durham; London: Duke University Press, 2013.

Fischer-Lichte, Erika. *The Transformative Power of Performance*. Abingdon: Routledge, 2008.

Fleetwood, Nicole R. *Troubling Vision: Performance, Visuality, and Blackness*. Chicago: The University of Chicago Press, 2011.

Fortuna, Victoria. *Moving Otherwise*. New York: Oxford University Press, 2019.

Fusco, Coco. 'The Other History of Intercultural Performance'. *TDR: The Drama Review* 38, no. 1 (Spring 1994): 143–167.

Fusco, Coco. *Corpus Delecti: Performance of the Americas*. Abingdon: Routledge, 2005.

Goffman, Erving. *The Presentation of Self in Everyday Life*. New York: Anchor Books, 1959.

Goldberg, RoseLee. *Performance: Live Art Since 1960*. London; New York: Thames & Hudson, 1998.

Goldberg, RoseLee. *Performance Art: From Futurism to the Present*. 3rd edn. World of Art. London; New York: Thames & Hudson, 2011.

Hamera, Judith. *Dancing Communities: Performance, Difference, and Connection in the Global City*. New York: Palgrave Macmillan, 2007.

Hamera, Judith. 'Performance Studies in Critical Communication Studies', in J. Nussbaum, ed., *Oxford Research Encyclopedia of Communication*. New York: Oxford University Press, 2018.

Harding, J., and C. Rosenthal, eds. *The Rise of Performance Studies: Rethinking Richard Schechner's Broad Spectrum*. Basingstoke: Palgrave Macmillan, 2011.

Hartman, Saidiya V. *Scenes of Subjection: Terror, Slavery, and Self-making in Nineteenth-century America*. New York: Oxford University Press, 1997.

Heathfield, Adrian, and Tehching Hsieh. *Out of Now: The Lifeworks of Tehching Hsieh*. London; Cambridge: MIT Press, 2009.

Hutcheon, Linda. *A Theory of Parody: The Teachings of Twentieth-century Art Forms*. New York: Methuen, 1985.

Jackson, Shannon. *Professing Performance: Theatre in the Academy from Philology to Performativity*. Cambridge: Cambridge University Press, 2004.

Johnson, E. Patrick. *Appropriating Blackness*. Durham: Duke University Press, 2003.

Johnson, E. Patrick. *Sweet Tea: Black Gay Men of the South*. Chapel Hill: University of North Carolina Press, 2008.

Johnson, E. Patrick. *Honeypot: Black Southern Women Who Love Women*. Durham: Duke University Press, 2019.

Johnson, E. Patrick, and Ramón H. Rivera-Servera. *Blacktino Queer Performance*. Durham: Duke University Press, 2016.

Jones, Amelia. *Body Art: Performing the Subject*. Minneapolis: University of Minnesota Press, 1998.

Jones, Omi Osun Joni L. *Theatrical Jazz: Performance, Àṣẹ, and the Power of the Present Moment. Black Performance and Cultural Criticism*. Columbus: Ohio State University Press, 2015.

Kershaw, Baz, and Helen Nicholson. *Research Methods in Theatre and Performance*. Edinburgh: Edinburgh University Press, 2011.

Knowles, Ric. 'Interspecies Performance'. *Theatre Journal* (Washington, DC) 65, no. 3 (2013).

Kuppers, Petra. *Disability, Arts and Culture: Methods and Approaches.* Bristol; Chicago: Intellect, 2019.

Lacan, Jacques. *The Four Fundamental Concepts of Psycho-Analysis.* 1st edn. London: Routledge, 1973.

Lyotard, Jean François. *The Postmodern Condition: A Report on Knowledge.* Minneapolis: University of Minnesota Press, 1984.

Madison, D. Soyini. *Performed Ethnography and Communication.* Taylor and Francis, 2018.

Madison, D. Soyini, and Judith Hamera. *The SAGE Handbook of Performance Studies.* Thousand Oaks: SAGE Publications, 2006.

Marcuse, Herbert. *Eros and Civilization: A Philosophical Inquiry into Freud.* Humanitas; Beacon Studies in Humanities. Boston: Beacon Press, 1955.

McKenzie, Jon. *Perform or Else: From Discipline to Performance.* London; New York: Routledge, 2001.

McKenzie, Jon, Roms Heike and C.J.W-L. Wee. *Contesting Performance. Performance Interventions.* Basingstoke: Palgrave Macmillan, 2009.

McMillan, Uri. *Embodied Avatars: Genealogies of Black Feminist Art and Performance.* Sexual Cultures: 5. New York: New York University Press, 2015.

Mitchell, Gregory. *Tourist Attractions: Performing Race and Masculinity in Brazil's Sexual Economy.* Chicago; London: The University of Chicago Press, 2016.

Moten, Fred. *In the Break: The Aesthetics of the Black Radical Tradition.* Minneapolis: University of Minnesota Press, 2003.

Mulvey, Laura. *Visual and Other Pleasures.* 2nd edn. New York: Palgrave Macmillan, 2009.

Muñoz, José Esteban. *Disidentifications: Queers of Color and the Performance of Politics.* Minneapolis; London: University of Minnesota Press, 1999.

Muñoz, José Esteban. *Cruising Utopia: The Then and There of Queer Futurity.* New York: New York University Press, 2009.

Muñoz, José Esteban. *The Sense of Brown.* Durham: Duke University Press, 2020.

Nyong'o, Tavia. *The Amalgamation Waltz: Race, Performance, and the Ruses of Memory.* Minneapolis: University of Minnesota Press, 2009.

Patraka, Vivian. *Spectacular Suffering: Theatre, Fascism, and the Holocaust.* Bloomington: Indiana University Press, 1999.

Phelan, Peggy. *Unmarked: The Politics of Performance.* New York; London: Routledge, 1993.

Phelan, Peggy, and Jill Lane. *The Ends of Performance.* New York: New York University Press, 1998.

Pollock, Della. *Telling Bodies Performing Birth: Everyday Narratives of Childbirth* New York: Columbia University Press, 1999.

Read, Alan. *Theatre, Intimacy and Engagement: The Last Human Venue.* Basingstoke: Palgrave Macmillan, 2007.

Reinelt, Janelle G., and Joseph Roach. *Critical Theory and Performance*. Ann Arbor: University of Michigan Press, 1992.

Roach, Joseph R. *Cities of the Dead: Circum-Atlantic Performance*. New York: Columbia University Press, 1996.

Román, David. *Acts of Intervention: Performance, Gay Culture, and AIDS*. Bloomington: Indiana University Press, 1998.

Rose, Gillian. *Visual Methodologies: An Introduction to the Interpretation of Visual Materials*. 2nd edn. London; Thousand Oaks: SAGE Publications, 2007.

Sandahl, Carrie, and Philip Auslander. *Bodies in Commotion. Corporealities*. Ann Arbor: University of Michigan Press, 2009.

Schechner, Richard. *Between Theatre & Anthropology*. Philadelphia: University of Pennsylvania Press, 1985.

Schechner, Richard. 'A New Paradigm for Theatre in the Academy'. *TDR: The Drama Review* 36, no. 4 (1992): 7–10.

Schechner, Richard. *Performed Imaginaries*. New York: Routledge, 2014.

Schneider, Rebecca. *The Explicit Body in Performance*. 1st edn. London; New York: Routledge, 1997.

Schneider, Rebecca. *Performing Remains: Art and War in Times of Theatrical Reenactment*. New York: Routledge, 2011.

Searle, John R. *Speech Acts: An Essay in the Philosophy of Language*. London: Cambridge University Press, 1969.

Sedgwick, Eve Kosofsky. *Touching Feeling: Affect, Pedagogy, Performativity*. Durham; London: Duke University Press, 2003.

Sikes, Alan. 'But Is it Theater? The Impact of Colonial Culture on Theatrical History in India', in Henry Bial and Scott Magelssen, eds, *Theater Historiography: Critical Interventions*. Ann Arbor: University of Michigan Press, 2010.

Spatz, Ben. *What a Body Can Do: Technique as Knowledge, Practice as Research*. Abingdon; New York: Routledge, 2015.

Striff, Erin. *Performance Studies. Readers in Cultural Criticism*. London: Macmillan Education, 2002.

Stucky, Nathan, and Cynthia Wimmer. *Teaching Performance Studies. Theater in the Americas*. Carbondale: Southern Illinois University Press, 2002.

Taylor, Diana. *The Archive and the Repertoire: Performing Cultural Memory in the Americas*. Durham; London: Duke University Press, 2003.

Taylor, Diana. *Performance*. Durham; London: Duke University Press, 2016.

Taylor, Diana. *¡Presente!: The Politics of Presence*. Durham; London: Duke University Press, 2020.

Teves, Stephanie Nohelani. 'The Theorist and the Theorized: Indigenous Critiques of Performance Studies'. *TDR: Drama Review* 62, no. 4 (2018): 131–140.

Thornham, Sue. *Feminist Film Theory*. Edinburgh: Edinburgh University Press, 1999.

Turner, Victor. *From Ritual to Theatre: The Human Seriousness of Play*. New York: Performing Arts Journal Publications, 1982.

Vazquez, Alexandra. *Listening in Detail: Performances of Cuban Music*. Durham: Duke University Press, 2013.

Wallis, Brian, Marianne Weems and Philip Yenawine, eds. *Art Matters: How the Culture Wars Changed America*. New York; London: New York University Press, 1999.

Wark, Jayne. *Radical Gestures: Feminism and Performance Art in North America*. Montreal; Ithaca: McGill–Queen's University Press, 2006.

Wilderson, Frank B. III. '"Raw Life" and the Ruse of Empathy', in P. Lichtenfels and J. Rouse, eds, *Performance, Politics, and Activism*. New York; Basingstoke: Palgrave Macmillan, 2013: 181–206.

Young, Harvey. 'Writing in Paint', in Henry Bial and Scott Magelssen, eds, *Theater Historiography: Critical Interventions*. Ann Arbor: University of Michigan Press, 2010.

Young, Harvey. *Embodying Black Experience. Theater: Theory / Text / Performance*. Ann Arbor: University of Michigan Press, 2010.

INDEX

Printed in the United States
by Baker & Taylor Publisher Services